Grade 5
Mathematics
Student Book 5A

PAT LILBURN
PETER SULLIVAN

in consultation with
Elsie Kinavai
Alex Feeger

Department of Education Papua New Guinea

AUSTRALIA & NEW ZEALAND

253 Normanby Road, South Melbourne, Victoria 3205, Australia

Oxford University Press is a department of the University of Oxford.
It furthers the University's objective of excellence in research,
scholarship, and education by publishing worldwide in

Oxford New York

Auckland Cape Town Dar es Salaam Hong Kong Karachi
Kuala Lumpur Madrid Melbourne Mexico City Nairobi
New Delhi Shanghai Taipei Toronto

With offices in

Argentina Austria Brazil Chile Czech Republic France Greece Guatemala
Hungary Italy Japan Poland Portugal Singapore South Korea Switzerland
Thailand Turkey Ukraine Vietnam

First published 2001
Reprinted 2003, 2008 (twice), 2009, 2010

ISBN 978 0 19 550865 9

Cover design by Sylvia Witte
Typesetting by Promptset Pty Ltd (Stephen Chan)
Cover artwork by Gigs Wena
Illustrated by Ophelia Leviny, Boris Sylvestri and Promptset Pty Ltd
Printed in China by Golden Cup Printing Co. Ltd
Published by Oxford University Press

Editorial Office: PO Box 7979, Boroko NCD, Papua New Guinea

Secretary's Message

This student book is part of the new reformed mathematics program designed and written for use in Grade 5 classes in Community Primary schools throughout Papua New Guinea.

The core materials consist of two student books called *Grade 5 Mathematics Student Book 5A* and *Grade 5 Mathematics Studen Book 5B*. They are accompanied by the *Grade 5 Mathematics Teacher's Resource Book*. They replace the MACS series now in use.

In the Mathematics program students are first taught mathematics by using real objects. Later, the students will use pictures of objects. Finally, the students will use number symbols to represent these objects. Always allow your students to use real objects dur their mathematics lessons if they want to. Teach the concepts in the context of real life situations as this leads to an appreciation of everyday use of mathematics skills and knowledge. The students will decide when they do not need the help of real objects any long Remember, when students use real objects, they will understand mathematics better. This program also encourages the students to solve their own problems and make their own decisions with confidence. In order to learn these skills, the students should talk abou what they are doing in every lesson. Since learning is most effective when it has meaning and is enjoyable, allow the students to us the language that they are most comfortable with.

However, in Grade 5 more English should be used together with the vernacular and other languages to aid understanding of ne and difficult concepts.

Finally, the National Department of Education wants teachers to be flexible in programming and timetabling to cater for the different abilities of students and multigrade teaching situations. This book shows you some strategies to help satisfy these needs.

Peter M. Baki

PETER M. BAKI
Secretary of Education

CONTENTS

Describing lengths

For questions 1 to 4, decide which of the statements best describes the length of the line. Do not use a ruler.

1. ________________________________

(a) between 1 cm and 4 cm
(b) between 4 cm and 7 cm
(c) Between 7 cm and 10 cm
(d) between 10 cm and 13 cm

2. ____

(a) between 5 cm and 1 m
(b) between 5 cm and 20 cm
(c) between 5 cm and 50 cm
(d) between 5 cm and 10 cm

3. __________

(a) less than 1 m
(b) less than 50 cm
(c) less than 10 cm
(d) less than 1 cm

4.

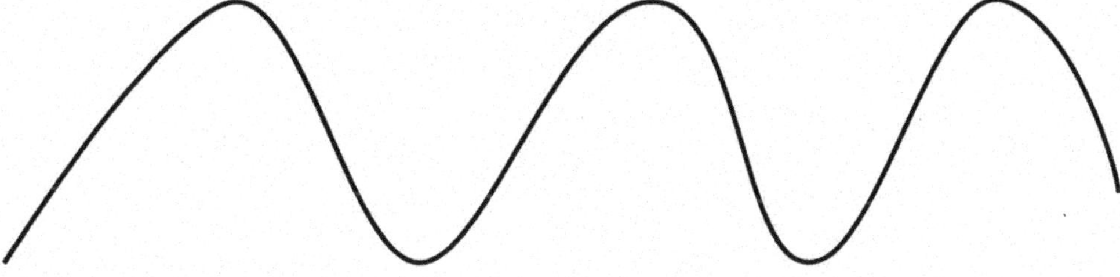

(a) more than 5 cm
(b) more than 15 cm
(c) more than 20 cm
(d) more than 30 cm

5. In your books draw lines that fit these descriptions:

(a) a straight line between 10 cm and 15 cm long
(b) a straight line between 3 cm and 4 cm long
(c) a rectangle that is less than 20 cm around
(d) a circle that is more than 20 cm around

6. ✎ **Challenge activity** ✎

On a single page of your book, write your name using a single unbroken line that is exactly 1 m long.

Writing lengths in different ways

1. Write these lengths using metres and centimetres
   e.g. 153 cm = 1m 53 cm

   (a) 280 cm
   (b) 500 cm
   (c) 325 cm
   (d) 115 cm
   (e) 1 250 cm
   (f) 680 cm
   (g) 2 500 cm
   (h) 3 825 cm

2. Write these lengths in centimetres
   e.g. 3 m 20 cm = 320 cm

   (a) 3 m 12 cm
   (b) 5 m 90 cm
   (c) 9 m 20 cm
   (d) 5 m 4 cm
   (e) 15 m 30 cm
   (f) 25 m 50 cm
   (g) 12 m 65 cm
   (h) 30 m 2 cm

3. Write these lengths using kilometres and metres
   e.g. 3 250 m = 3 km 250 cm

   (a) 1 500 m
   (b) 7 800 m
   (c) 3 124 m
   (d) 8 250 m
   (e) 12 250 m
   (f) 15 000 m
   (g) 23 500 m
   (h) 52 600 m

4. Write these lengths in metres
   e.g. 2 km 250 m = 2 250 m

   (a) 3 km 150 m
   (b) 4 km 500 m
   (c) 12 km
   (d) 15 km 500 m
   (e) 8 km 200 m
   (f) 1 km 10 m
   (g) 28 km 200 m
   (h) 17 km 50 m

Measuring perimeters

1. If each of the squares in this grid is 1 cm long and 1 cm wide, what is the perimeter of these shaded figures?

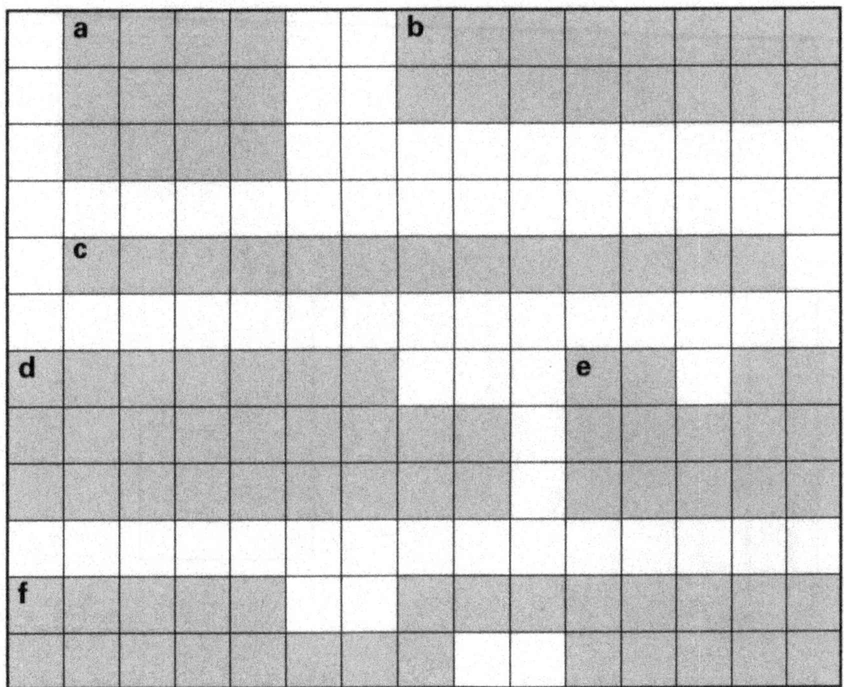

2. As accurately as possible, measure the perimeter of these shapes in cm.

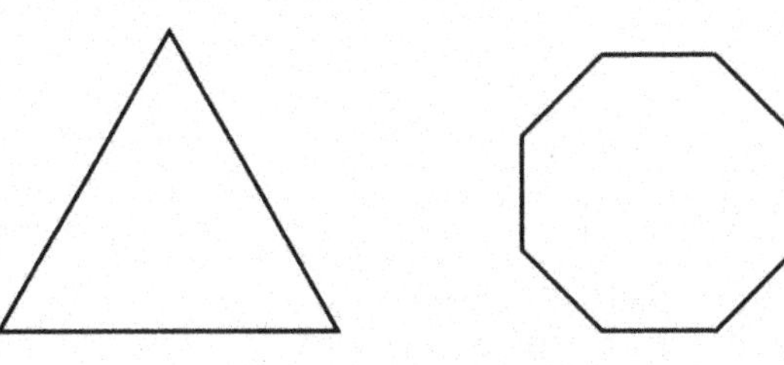

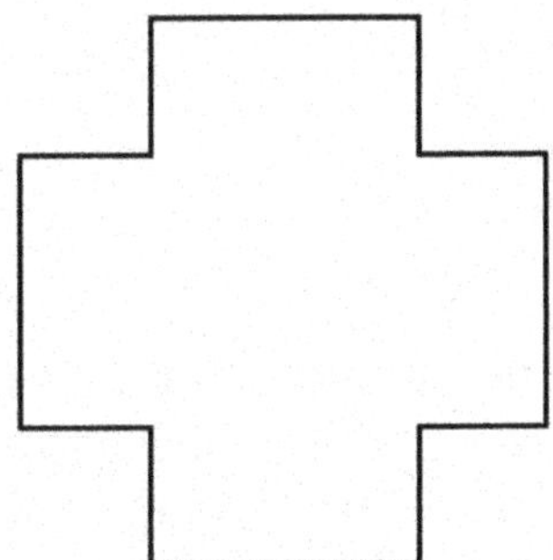

3. Draw some shapes that have a perimeter of 12 cm.

Calculating perimeters

1. Each of the following diagrams represents someone's garden. What is the perimeter of each of these gardens?

(a)

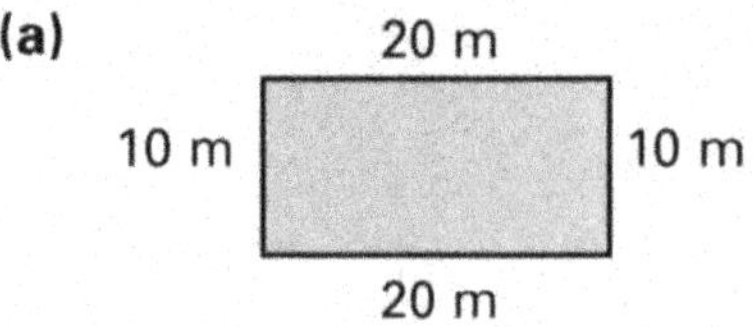

(b)

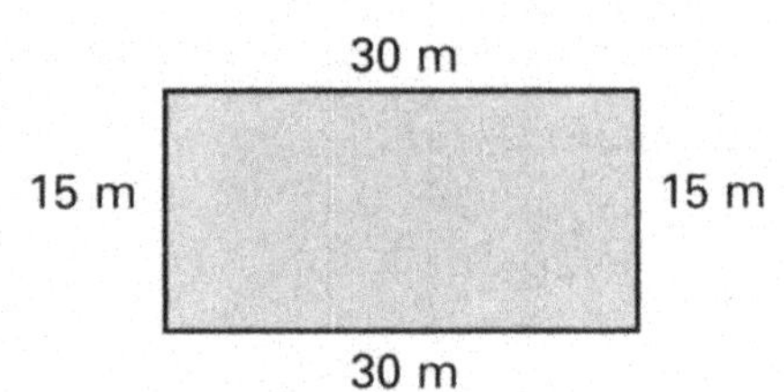

(c)

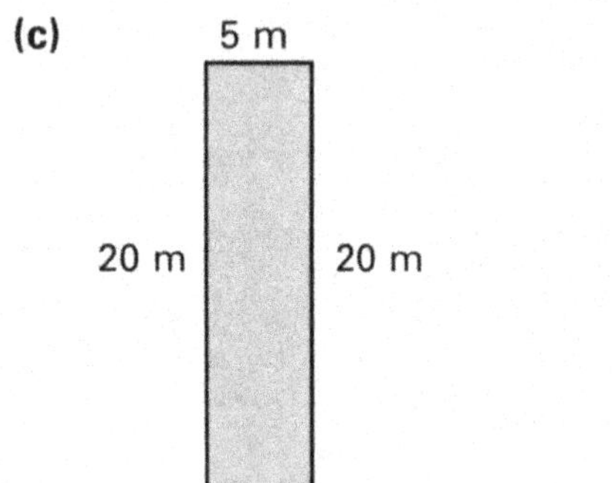

(d)

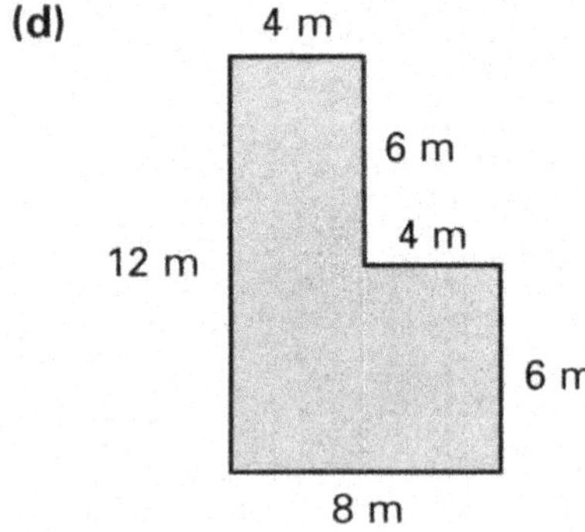

(e)

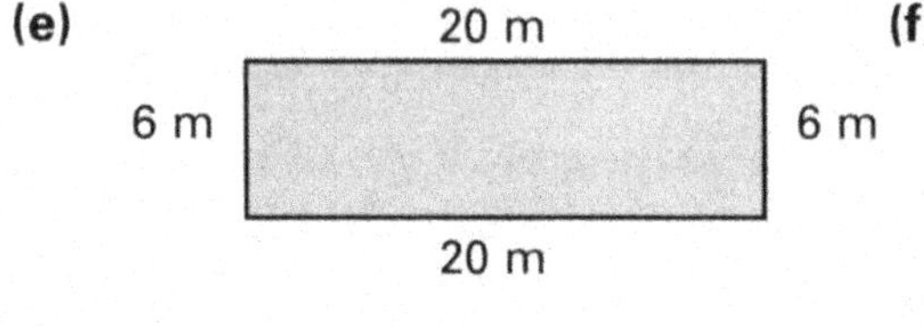

(f)

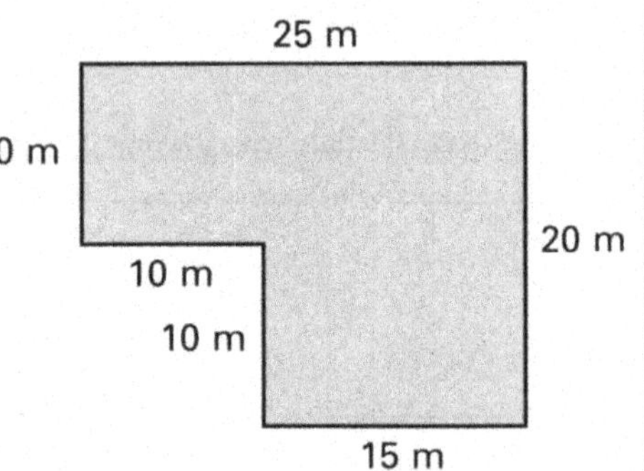

2. Draw a diagram to represent a garden that:

(a) is the shape of a rectangle with a perimeter of 30 m
(b) is the shape of a rectangle with a perimeter of 24 m
(c) is an 'L' shape with a perimeter of 36 m
(d) is an 'L' shape with a perimeter of 40 m

Solving length problems

1. I want to cover a wall that is 10 m wide with woven blinds. I have some woven blinds that are 1 m, 2 m, 3 m, 4 m, and 5 m wide. Which pieces could I use?

2. I want to build a fence that is 50 m long. Each 5 m of fence needs two rails that are 5 m long, and the fence posts are 5 m apart. How many rails and how many posts do I need?

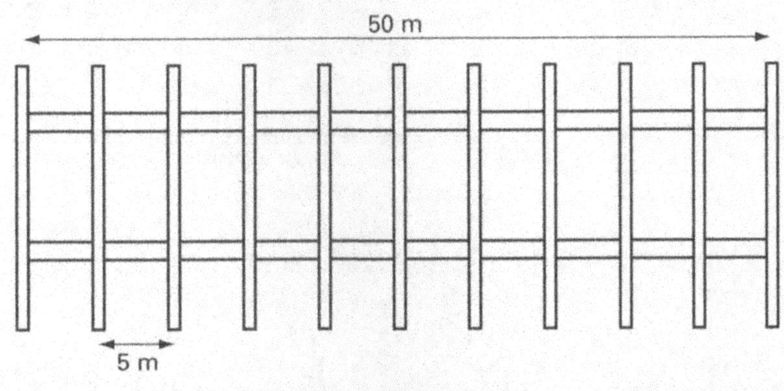

3. Draw a shape that has 4 sides, with sides that are 6 cm, 7 cm, 8 cm and 9 cm.

4. Draw a circle that is between 20 cm and 25 cm around.

5. Draw a triangle that has a perimeter between 10 cm and 12 cm.

6. How tall is your school flagpole?

7. How much longer is your arm span than your height?

8. How many different rectangles can you draw that have a perimeter of 16 cm?

9. A rectangle has the length 10 cm longer than the width. Its perimeter is 100 cm. What is the length and width?

10. A rectangle is twice as long as it is wide. Its perimeter is 60 cm. What is its length and width?

What century?

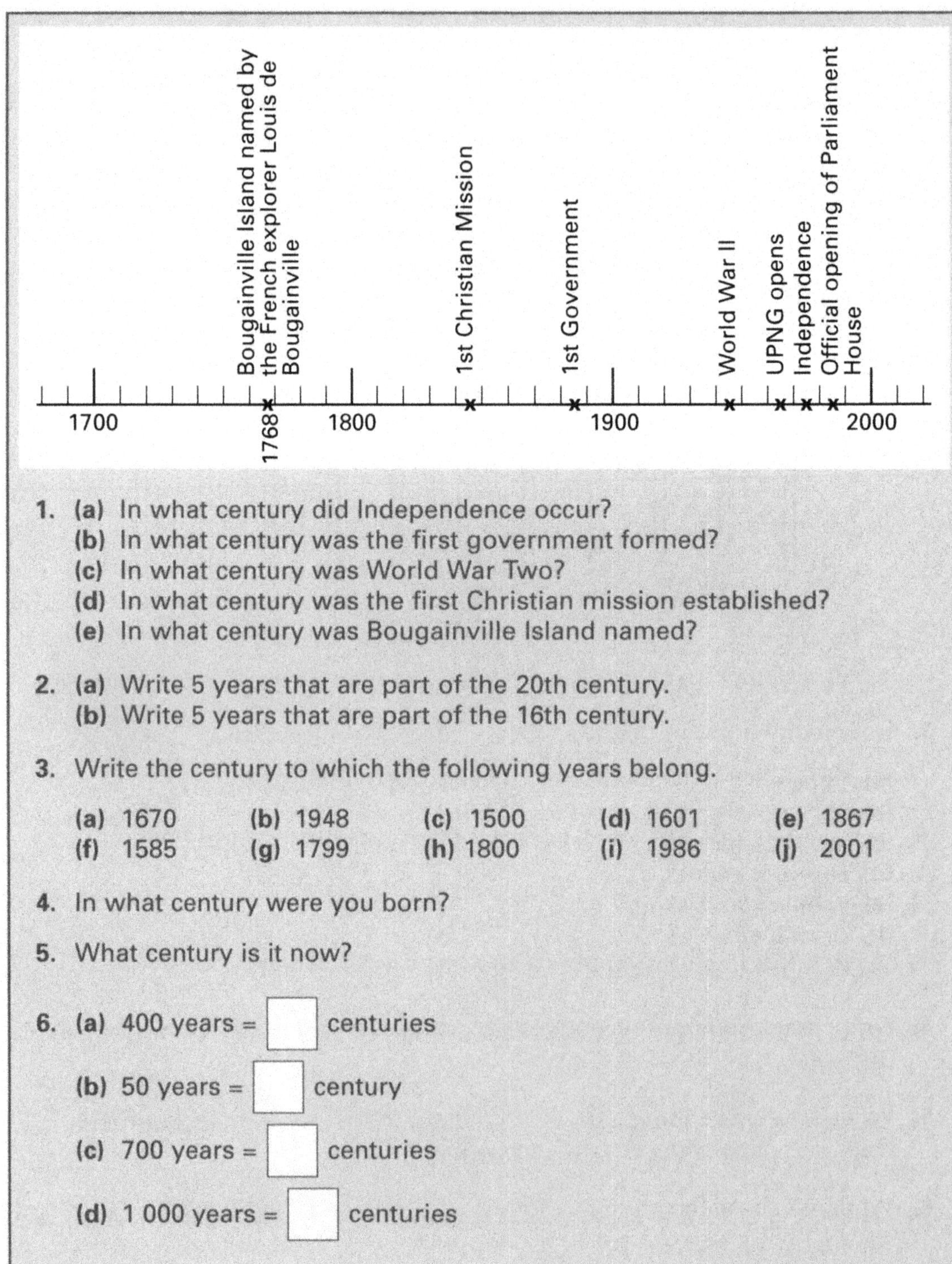

1. (a) In what century did Independence occur?
   (b) In what century was the first government formed?
   (c) In what century was World War Two?
   (d) In what century was the first Christian mission established?
   (e) In what century was Bougainville Island named?
2. (a) Write 5 years that are part of the 20th century.
   (b) Write 5 years that are part of the 16th century.
3. Write the century to which the following years belong.

(a) 1670	(b) 1948	(c) 1500	(d) 1601	(e) 1867
(f) 1585	(g) 1799	(h) 1800	(i) 1986	(j) 2001

4. In what century were you born?
5. What century is it now?
6. (a) 400 years = ☐ centuries

   (b) 50 years = ☐ century

   (c) 700 years = ☐ centuries

   (d) 1 000 years = ☐ centuries

Timing events

1. Estimate and then do each activity to find out how many seconds it takes to:

    (a) write your first name
    (b) jump 10 times
    (c) run 50 metres
    (d) say 'Papua New Guinea' 5 times
    (e) say a favourite rhyme

2. Who came first? Who came last?

3. How many times can you do each of these in 30 seconds?

    (a) jumps
    (b) finger clicks
    (c) say the alphabet
    (d) say your name
    (e) walk across your room
    (f) draw a circle

4. Find some activities that take exactly 10 seconds to do.

5. What are some things that take close to 1 minute to do?

6. What are some things that take close to 1 hour to do?

Time facts

1. How many seconds in:

   (a) 1 minute? (b) 2 minutes? (c) 5 minutes?

   (d) 10 minutes? (e) $1\frac{1}{2}$ minutes? (f) $2\frac{1}{4}$ minutes?

2. How many minutes in:

   (a) 1 hour? (b) 5 hours? (c) 10 hours?

   (d) $\frac{1}{2}$ hour? (e) $2\frac{1}{2}$ hours? (f) $1\frac{1}{4}$ hours?

3. How many hours in:

   (a) 1 day? (b) 2 days? (c) 5 days?

   (d) $\frac{1}{2}$ day? (e) $1\frac{1}{2}$ days? (f) 10 days?

4. How many days in:

   (a) 1 week? (b) 2 weeks? (c) 10 weeks?
   (d) 5 weeks? (e) 8 weeks? (f) 15 weeks?

5. How many days in:

   (a) 1 fortnight? (b) 3 fortnights? (c) 7 fortnights?
   (d) 10 fortnights? (e) 5 fortnights? (f) 15 fortnights?

6. How many times does the hour hand pass the 12 in 5 days?

7. A woman was paid K5 per hour for an 8 hour day. The job took $3\frac{1}{2}$ days to complete. How much was she paid?

8. How many seconds are there in 3 hours?

Digital and clock times

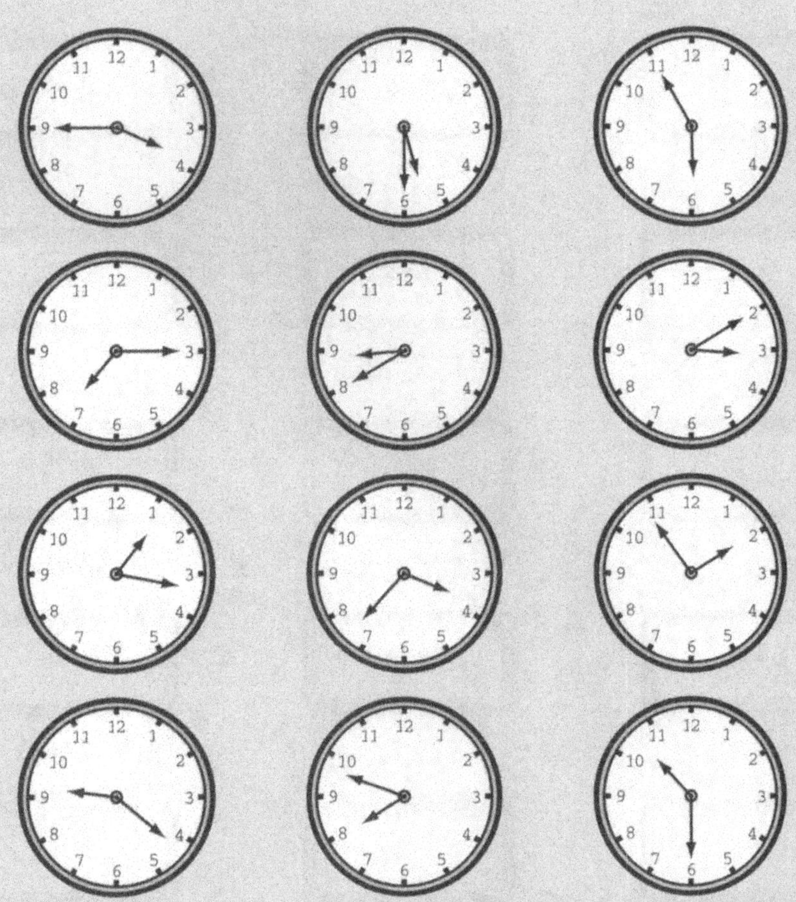

1. Write the time shown as both digital and clock times.
2. Write the time that each clock will show two hours later.
3. Write the time that each clock will show 30 minutes earlier.
4. Work out how long each clock has until the hands reach midnight. (All times shown are p.m. times.)
5. Work out which clock is closest to

   (a) 6 o'clock **(b)** 2 o'clock **(c)** 1:30 **(d)** 4:15
6. This time, read the clocks as a.m. times. Put them in order from the earliest time to the latest time.

Relating digital and clock times

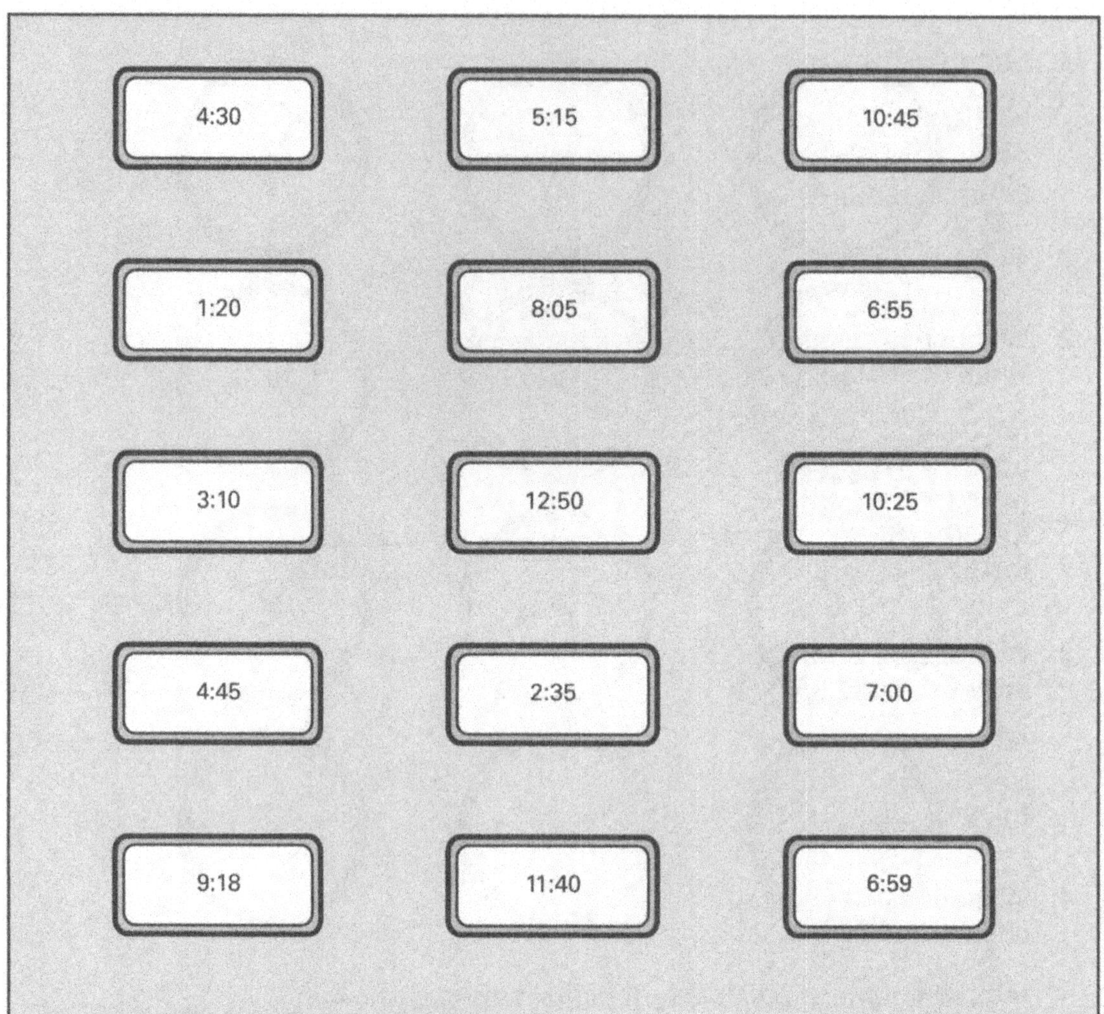

For each of the digital times shown:

1. Write the time, as you would read it on a clock. Then draw a clock to show each time.

2. Write the digital time that is 15 minutes after the time shown.

3. Write the digital time that is 15 minutes before the time shown.

4. Write the time that is 6 hours after, 3 hours after, and 10 hours after the time shown.

Odds and evens

1. From this list, write down in your books the even numbers.

869	2 401	12 869
327	8 679	21 689
896	2 140	31 427
432	3 145	38 668
423	8 769	30 889

2. Without calculating, which of the additions will give an odd answer? Write the letter in your book.

(a) 34 + 25	**(b)** 35 + 67	**(c)** 29 + 82
(d) 82 + 47	**(e)** 35 + 35	**(f)** 44 + 82
(g) 53 + 91	**(h)** 77 + 88	**(i)** 49 + 99
(j) 36 + 46	**(k)** 329 + 429	**(l)** 537 + 884
(m) 622 + 378	**(n)** 286 + 395	**(o)** 415 + 415

3. Without calculating, which of these subtraction tasks will give an odd answer? Write the letter in your book.

(a) 52 – 42	**(b)** 52 – 34	**(c)** 63 – 21
(d) 73 – 57	**(e)** 84 – 31	**(f)** 84 – 69
(g) 91 – 34	**(h)** 91 – 58	**(i)** 120 – 32

4. Without calculating, which of these multiplications will give an even answer? Write the letter in your book.

(a) 8 x 4	**(b)** 26 x 3	**(c)** 51 x 6
(d) 13 x 11	**(e)** 21 x 5	**(f)** 22 x 32
(g) 56 x 56	**(h)** 27 x 4	**(i)** 8 x 17

5. Write down what you notice about the even numbered pages in this book. Is the same true for other books?

6. **Challenge activity**

In groups discuss the following problem. Five numbers add together to make an odd number. What can you say about the numbers?

Numbers in rectangles

I have 6 square tiles. They can be arranged to make some rectangles. For example,

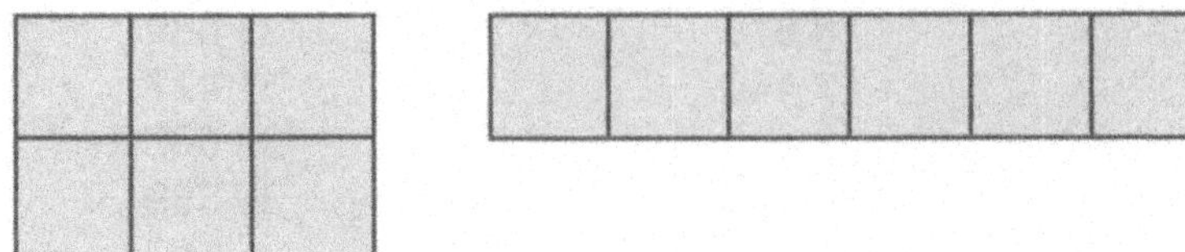

1. In your book, draw as many rectangles as you can using 20 squares.
2. Draw as many rectangles as you can using 16 square tiles.
3. Draw as many rectangles as you can using 36 square tiles.
4. 18 children want to form into equal groups. What groups are possible?
5. 25 children want to dance in equal groups. What groups are possible?
6. 24 children want to play sport.
   What size teams are possible?
   What sports could the children play?
7. 48 children want to arrange themselves in equal groups. What groups are possible?
8. Draw as many rectangles as you can using 27 square tiles.
9. Draw as many rectangles as you can using 13 square tiles.
   How is this answer different from the previous answers?
   What other numbers are like 13?
10. 30 children want to play sport. Basketball needs 5 players, volleyball needs 6 players, softball needs 9 players and 11 players are needed for soccer. For which sports could these children form teams so that all of the children are in a team?
11. Some children in a school arranged themselves in groups of 6. There were no children left over. How many children could there be in the school?

Multiples and factors

1. Copy this table into your book. Complete the missing squares.

Multiples

2	4	6	8	10	12	14	16	18	20
3	6	9	12						
4	8	12							
5									
6									
7									
8									
9									
10									

2. Using the table:

   (a) Write down those numbers that are multiples of both 2 and 5.
   (b) Write down those numbers that are multiples of 3 and 4.
   (c) What is the smallest number that is a multiple of both 5 and 6?
   (d) What is the smallest number that is a multiple of both 2 and 3?

3. What are some numbers that have both 4 and 5 as factors?

4. What are some numbers that have both 3 and 5 as factors?

5. In Warupolo village eggs are tied in leaf bundles of 3. Four of these bundles are tied to a stick for carrying. Which of the following numbers of eggs will give whole 'sticks' with no leftovers? 12, 16, 24, 28, 32.

6. What are some numbers that have exactly 4 factors?

7. Copy and fill in the missing numbers.

Product	24	18	21	22	36
Factor		6		11	
Factor	6		3		

Product			24	
Factor	1	3		10
Factor		10	2	
Factor	13			

8. ✎ **Challenge activity** ✎

I am an odd number.
My digits add to 6.

What numbers could I be?
What numbers could I be a multiple of?
What numbers could I be if I am an even number?

Hundreds grid

In your books draw a grid like the one below but all the way to 200.

1	2	3	4	5	6	7	8	9	10
11	12	13	14	15	16	17	18	19	20
21	22	23	24	25	26	27			
31	32	33	34	35					
41	42	43	44						
51	52	53							
61	62								
71									
81									
91									
101									
111									

1. Colour in all the multiples of 2, EXCEPT 2.
   Write down what you notice about the numbers you coloured in.
2. Using a different colour, colour in the multiples of 5, EXCEPT 5, and the multiples of 10, EXCEPT 10.
   Write down what you notice about these patterns.
3. Repeat, using different colours, for the multiples of:
   4, EXCEPT 4
   8, EXCEPT 8
   3, EXCEPT 3
   6, EXCEPT 6
   9, EXCEPT 9
   7, EXCEPT 7
   Write down what you notice about these patterns.

Investigating 3's

28	246	3 720	36 214
65	617	4 193	25 210
37	821	8 825	32 488
41	535	4 016	56 732
80	912	5 027	39 817
19	302	5 139	10 050
16	810	5 826	12 360
22	413	3 716	14 927
35	751	9 250	86 513
60	816	9 106	92 777
89	555	2 612	

1. Without dividing, write down the multiples of 2 from the number lists above.

2. Without dividing, write down the multiples of 3.

3. Without dividing, write down the multiples of 5.

4. Without dividing, write down the multiples of 6.

5. Without dividing, write down the multiples of 10.

6. Which of these numbers are multiples of both 2 **and** 3?

7. Which of these numbers are multiples of both 2 **and** 5?

8. Which of these numbers are multiples of both 3 **and** 5?

Prime numbers

1. Write down all factors of these numbers.

9	64
15	69
17	47
27	32
37	23
48	51

2. What are some numbers that have 2 **and** 3 as factors?

3. What are some numbers that have 3 **and** 5 as factors?

4. 2, 3 and 5 are factors of a number. What could that number be? Give more than one answer.

5. Which of these numbers are prime numbers?

80	85
81	86
82	87
83	88
84	89

6. Which of these are prime numbers?

101	106
102	107
103	108
104	109
105	110

7. A *prime factor* is a factor which is also a prime number. What are the prime factors of these numbers?

9	55
15	60
17	100
27	360
32	200

Ordering numbers

1. Write as many numbers as you can that are between

   (a) 30 and 35 (b) 300 and 305 (c) 3 000 and 3 010
   (d) 65 and 75 (e) 605 and 615 (f) 6 010 and 6 015

2.. Write at least 5 numbers that are between

   (a) 280 and 320 (b) 3 900 and 4 100 (c) 250 and 450
   (d) 4 000 and 6 000 (e) 670 and 830 (f) 8 770 and 9 100

3. Write in order from largest to smallest.

   (a) 546, 578, 564, 506, 576
   (b) 2 567, 2 657, 2 576, 2 507, 2 756
   (c) 5 076, 5 067, 5 607, 5 760, 5 077

4. Write in order from smallest to largest.

   (a) 720, 702, 207, 270, 27
   (b) 5 243, 5 432, 5 234, 5 423
   (c) 7 094, 7 054, 8 504, 8 405

5. The following points were scores in a game.

Tau	2 768 points
Tagu	2 806 points
Tabo	2 788 points
Timu	2 466 points

   Write the names of the students in order from highest score to lowest score.

6. In Enga Province the annual rainfall in various places is as follows.

Kandep	2 489 mm
Kompiam	3 421 mm
Laiagan	2 162 mm
Porgera	3 095 mm
Wabong	3 015 mm
Wapenamanda	2 488 mm

   Write the places in order from lowest to highest rainfall.

Which one is different?

From each of these sets of numbers, choose one number that you think is different. Write your reasons for choosing this number.

(a) 3, 6, 9, 13

(b) 4, 7, 12, 6

(c) 10, 20, 35, 19

(d) 4, 9, 25, 20

(e) 3, 7, 9, 11

(f) 20, 24, 28, 26

(g) 15, 16, 17, 18

(h) 30, 31, 32, 33

(i) 5, 9, 11, 15

(j) 2 000, 200, 20, 10

Comparing angles

1. Which is the bigger angle out of each pair?

2. Write down the letters of these angles from largest to smallest.

3. Write down the letters of these angles from largest to smallest.

4. Write down the letters of these angles from largest to smallest.

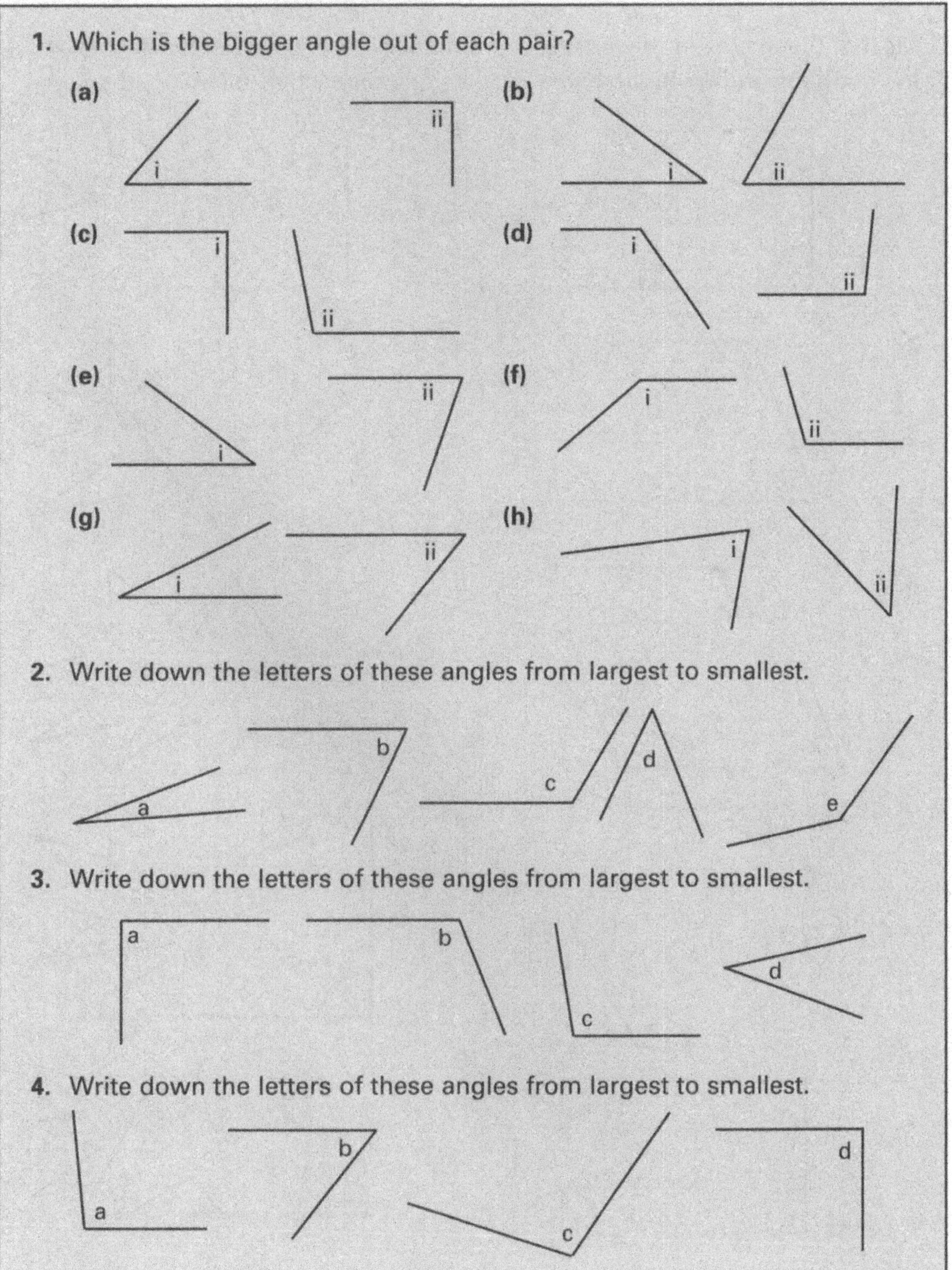

Angles in shapes

Most of the angles in these shapes are marked. Draw each of these shapes in your book and write the name of the angle on each of the marked angles.

1.

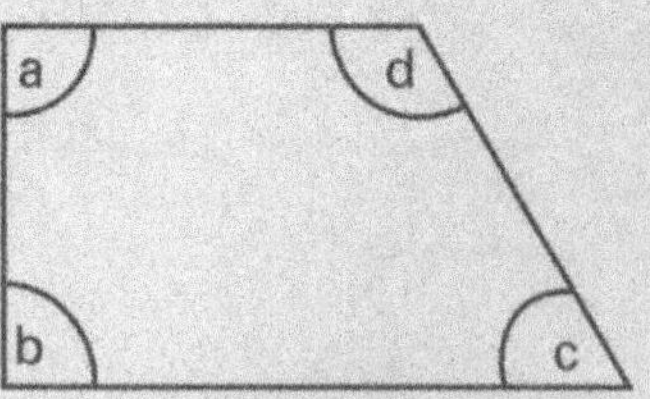

2.

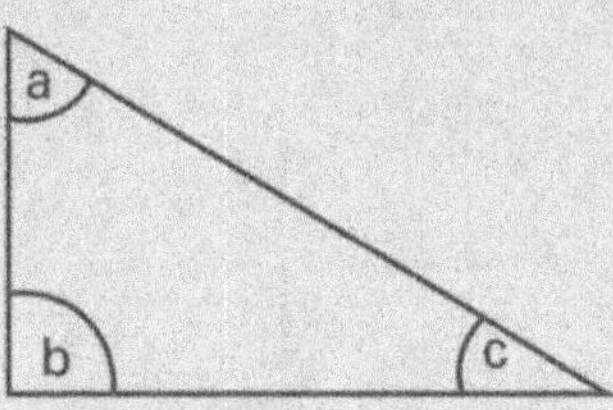

3.

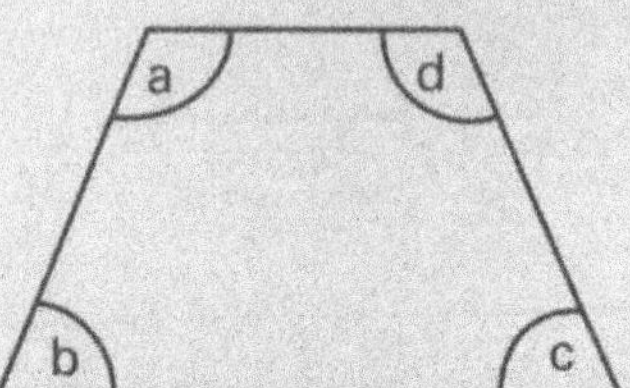

4.

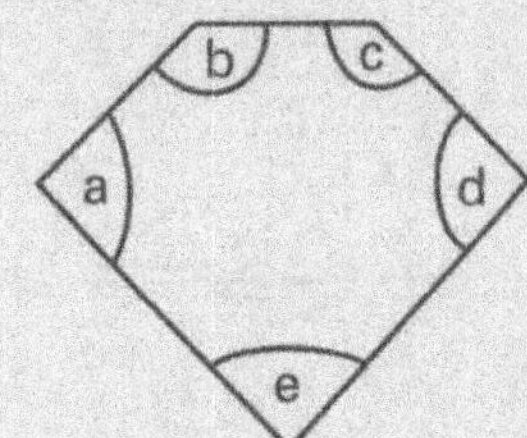

5.

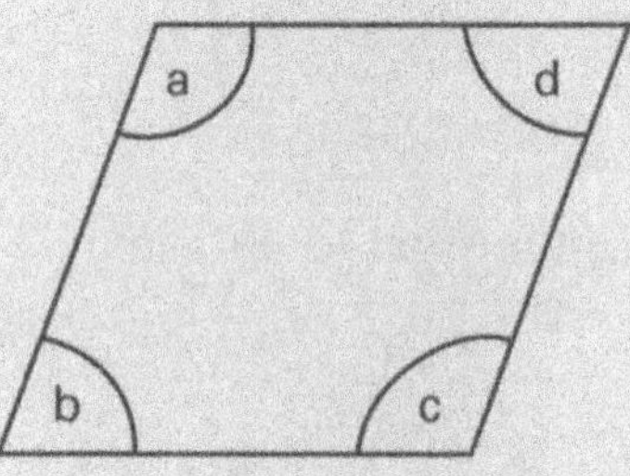

6.

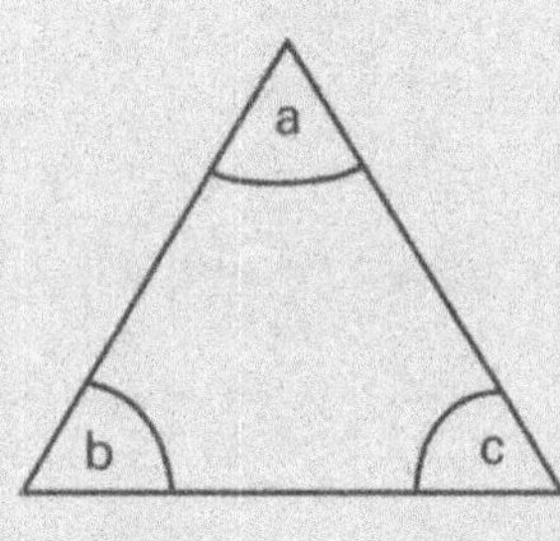

7.

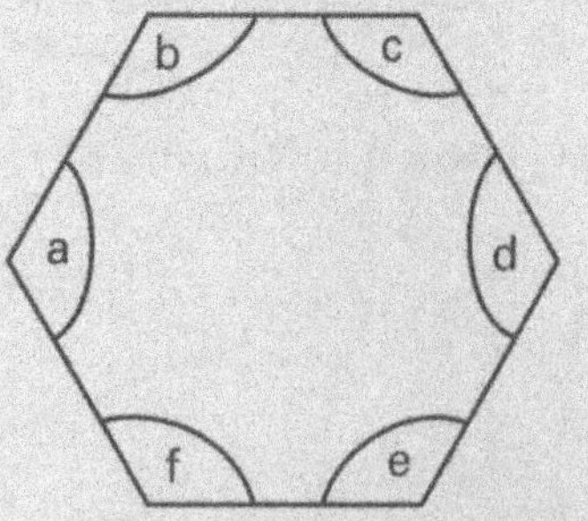

8.

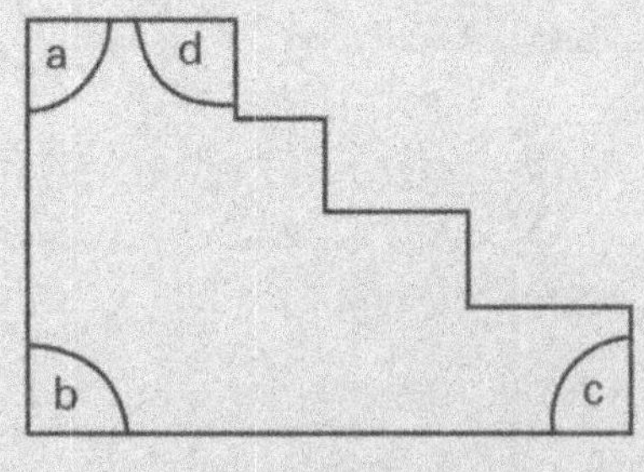

9.

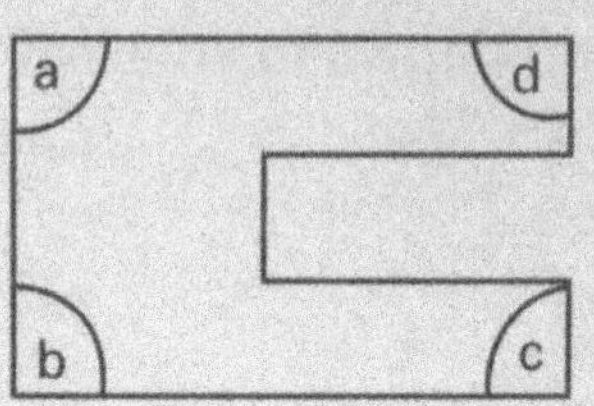

10.

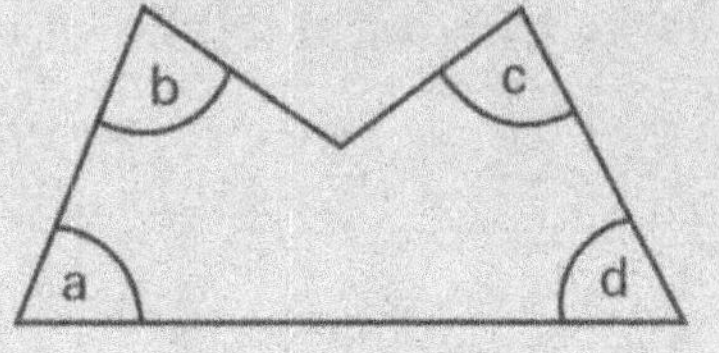

Map of Goroka

1. What is something due North of the airport?
2. What direction do you walk to go from the swimming pool to the post office?
3. What is South–West of the national park?
4. There is a school South of the hospital. What is the name of the school?
5. What are the names of some roads that run East–West?
6. What are the names of some roads that run North–South?
7. Give directions how to walk from Gouna Plaza to the museum. (It is not possible to walk across the airport.)
8. Give directions how to walk from the High School to the swimming pool.

Angle problems

Name the type of angle formed in each of the following (e.g. acute, right, obtuse, straight):

1. The angle you need to turn, to turn on the tap of a water tank.
2. The angle you need to turn a door handle to open a door.
3. The angle you turn a door to open it.
4. (a) The angle your body makes when you are sitting up straight in a chair.
   (b) The angle your body makes when you are lying flat on the ground.

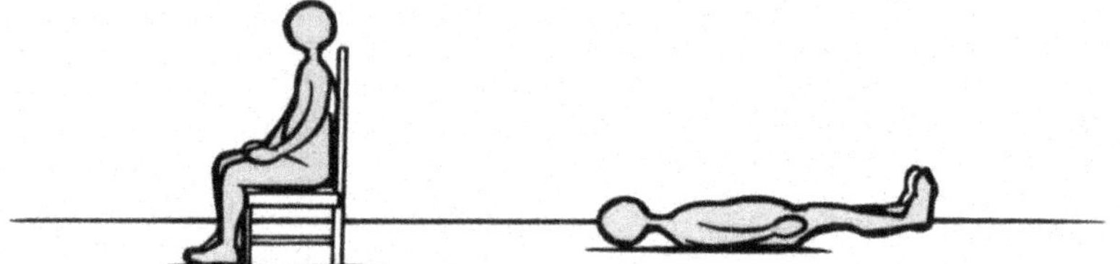

5. The angle you turn a light switch to turn the light on.
6. The angle you can spin around on one foot.
7. The angle you can turn your head from one extreme to the other.
8. The largest angle you can make between your thumb and first finger.

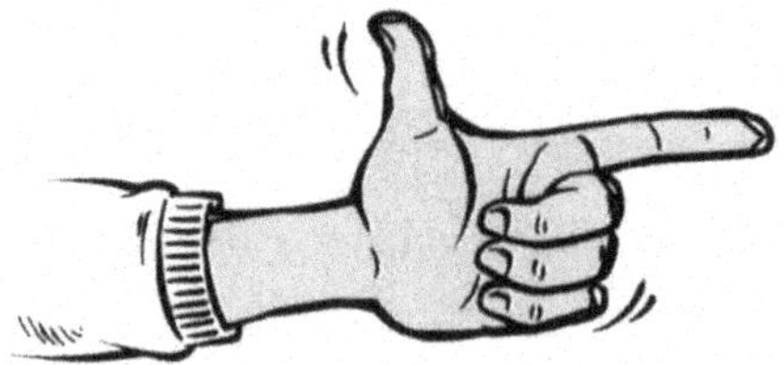

9. The angle grass bends in the wind.
10. The angle of your vision when sitting with your head still.
11. The angle of your vision when you are sitting, and moving your head.
12. Describe all of the angles the road leading to your school makes.
13. The angle that a person makes with a paddle when paddling in a canoe.
14. The angles between the toes of a chicken.

Scoreboard numbers

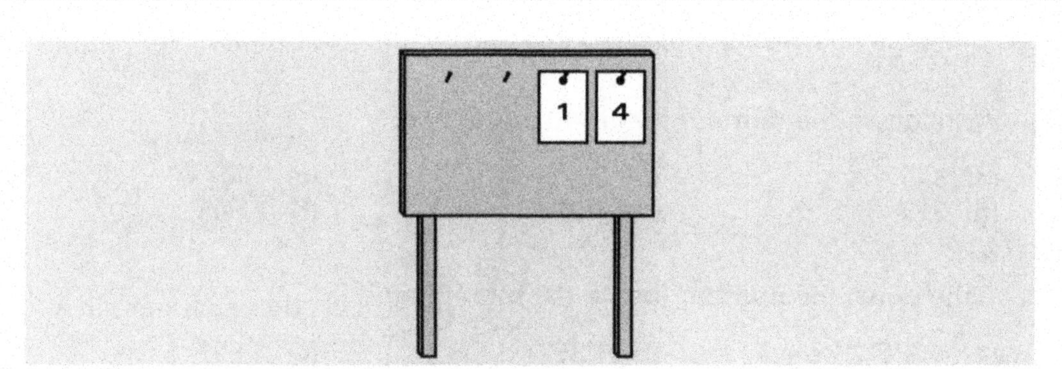

1. What is the score shown on this scoreboard?
2. Using only the number cards shown, list all the scores you can show.

(a) 3 7

(b) 3 5 7

(c) 3 7 8

(d) 9 0 5

(e) 2 3 7 1

(f) 2 7 5 1

(g) 2 4 7 2

(h) 1 0 1 4

3. ✎ Challenge activity ✎

If you wanted to use this scoreboard to show all the different times of the day, how many number cards would you need?

Short cuts for adding

Calculate the answer in your head, then write it in your book.

1. Write down the number that is 10 more than:

(a) 37	(b) 52	(c) 196
(d) 213	(e) 1 237	(f) 2 905

2. Write down the number that is 100 more than:

(a) 1 376	(b) 1 852	(c) 1 827
(d) 2 013	(e) 2 967	(f) 3 914

3. Write down the number 100 less than:

(a) 376	(b) 482	(c) 2 619
(d) 2 347	(e) 3 123	(f) 9 600

4. Write down the number that is 9 more than:

(a) 47	(b) 62	(c) 396
(d) 513	(e) 3 237	(f) 5 905

5. Write down the number that is 99 more than:

(a) 324	(b) 513	(c) 2 376
(d) 4 852	(e) 23 519	(f) 43 162

6. Write down the numbers 1 000 more than:

(a) 3 417	(b) 2 692	(c) 13 456
(d) 27 100	(e) 32 000	(f) 60 000

7. Write down the number 1 000 less than:

(a) 3 417	(b) 2 692	(c) 13 456
(d) 27 100	(e) 32 000	(f) 60 000

8. Write down the most important thing to think about when adding numbers like 10, 100, 1 000.

Numbers in places

1. Write down eleven different numbers each with a 7 in the **tens** place.

2. Write down eleven different numbers each with a 5 in the **hundreds** place.

3. Write down eleven different numbers each with a 3 in the **thousands** place.

4. Write down eleven different numbers each with a 2 in the **units** place and a 4 in the **tens** place.

5. Write down eleven different numbers each with a 2 in the **tens** place and a 7 in the **hundreds** place.

6. I am a 3 digit number. I have a 5 in the **tens** place. My **units** is even and bigger than 3. My **hundreds** is 7. What numbers might I be?

7. I am a 4 digit number. The sum of my digits is 11. My **tens** and **units** digits are odd. My **hundreds** digit is 2 and my thousands digit is a prime number. What numbers might I be?

8. I have a car number plate. It has a 3 in the **tens** place. What might the number plate be?

9. A plane flew overhead. It had a number on the wing. The number had a 3 in the **units** place. The tens number was bigger. What could the number of the plane be?

10. I am a three digit number. My units are 9. My tens are 4 less. The sum of my digits is 15. What number am I?

11. I am a three digit number. Each of my digits is a factor of six. The sum of my digits is 11. What digits am I made up of? What numbers could I be?

12. Write down five numbers, each with a zero in the hundreds place.

Rounding

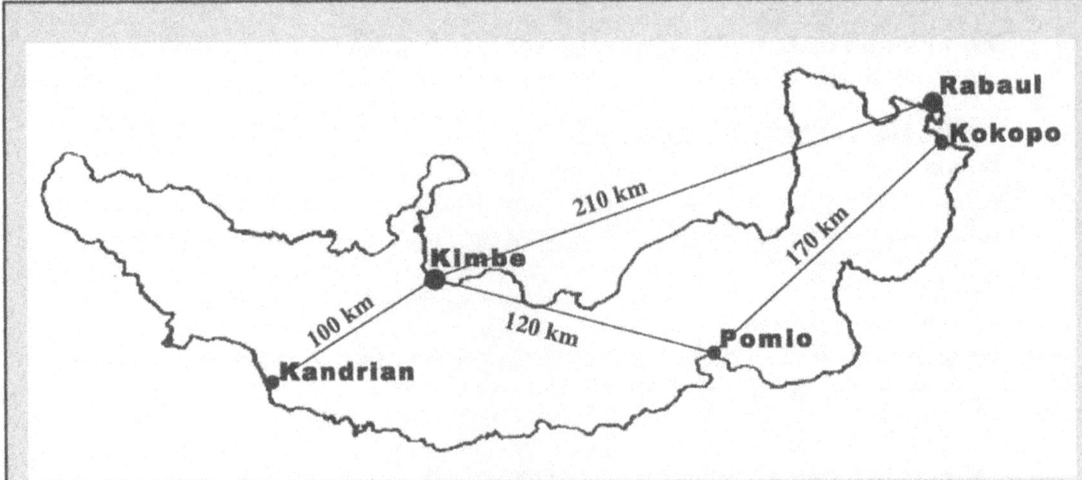

1. Round to the nearest 10:

   (a) 34 (b) 72 (c) 27
   (d) 86 (e) 65 (f) 44
   (g) 271 (h) 365 (i) 227
   (j) 3 461 (k) 2 998 (l) 3 004

2. Sometimes when rounding distances on a map, we need to know to the nearest 100 km. Round these numbers to the nearest 100 km.

   (a) 327 km (b) 591 km (c) 476 km
   (d) 551 km (e) 322 km (f) 818 km
   (g) 899 km (h) 902 km (i) 951 km
   (j) 3 461 km (k) 8 677 km (l) 5 040 km

3. When recording the volume of containers sometimes the numbers are rounded to the nearest 100 mL. Round these numbers to the nearest 100 mL.

   (a) 1 464 mL (b) 2 873 mL (c) 2 547 mL
   (d) 2 365 mL (e) 8 876 mL (f) 992 mL
   (g) 4 057 mL (h) 3 208 mL (i) 6 270 mL
   (j) 2 213 mL (k) 2 007 mL (l) 6 005 mL

4. A number is rounded to 660. What could it be?

5. A number is rounded to 6 000. What could the number be?

Reading and writing numbers in words

1. These invoices show the amount of money owed to Bilas Bakery. For each invoice, write the amount of kina in words, in your book.

	Bilas Bakery Invoice 675	16.02.01
To:	Joe Kila	
Amount:	______________________	K32.00

	Bilas Bakery Invoice 580	12.01.01
To:	Sila Suru	
Amount:	______________________	K308.00

	Bilas Bakery Invoice 810	23.03.02
To:	Rabe Primary School	
Amount:	______________________	K2001.00

	Bilas Bakery Invoice 770	03.03.02
To:	Mea Naru	
Amount:	______________________	K1290.00

2. These cheques show the amount of money in words. For each cheque, write the amount of kina in numbers, in your book.

(a) twenty-seven

Westpac bank - PNG - Limited 90326
WAIGANI *October 24 2002*
Pay *P.Sapias* or bearer
the sum of *Twenty-seven Kina only* K
07 0 00 076- 0 Jan Kendi

(b) one hundred and thirty nine

Westpac bank - PNG - Limited 90326
WAIGANI *October 24 2002*
Pay *S. MaKana* or bearer
the sum of *One hundred and thirty-nine Kina only* K
07 0 00 077- 0 John Kahulu

(c) five hundred and sixteen

Westpac bank - PNG - Limited 90326
WAIGANI *October 24 2002*
Pay *C.H.Chui* or bearer
the sum of *Five hundred and sixteen Kina only* K
07 0 00 078- 0 Sam Suneo

(d) two thousand, three hundred and ninety-six

Westpac bank - PNG - Limited 90326
WAIGANI *October 24 2002*
Pay *Piamba Estates* or bearer
the sum of *Two thousand, three hundred and ninety-six Kina only* K
07 0 00 079- 0 Maggie Thompson

(e) three thousand and fifty

Westpac bank - PNG - Limited 90326
WAIGANI *October 24 2002*
Pay *Maru Trading LTD* or bearer
the sum of *Three thousand and fifty Kina only* K
07 0 00 0710- 0 Heron Tineme

(f) sixty-seven thousand, three hundred and twenty-five

Westpac bank - PNG - Limited 90326
WAIGANI *October 24 2002*
Pay *N. Siau* or bearer
the sum of *Sixty-seven thousand, three hundred and twenty-five Kina* K
07 0 00 0711- 0 Alice Jengdui

Estimating and counting large groups

Estimate, then devise a way to count the number of objects in the following sets.

Addition your way

Copy the questions into your books and write the answer as a number sentence (**do the calculation in your head**).
e.g. 220 + 100 = 320

1. **(a)** 324 + 100 **(b)** 476 + 100
(c) 245 + 99 **(d)** 709 + 99
(e) 1 279 + 100 **(f)** 1 386 + 100
(g) 2 417 + 99 **(h)** 3 529 + 99

2. **(a)** 476 + 20 **(b)** 327 + 20
(c) 437 + 50 **(d)** 312 + 50
(e) 1 277 + 20 **(f)** 8 251 + 20
(g) 3 040 + 50 **(h)** 2 197 + 50

3. **(a)** 872 + 101 **(b)** 426 + 101
(c) 262 + 101 **(d)** 357 +101
(e) 283 + 200 **(f)** 631 + 200
(g) 535 + 200 **(h)** 901 + 200

4. **(a)** 327 + 251 **(b)** 314 + 461
(c) 273 + 316 **(d)** 2 161 + 307
(e) 2 534 + 1 325 **(f)** 8 271 + 1 006
(g) 251 + 1 327 **(h)** 307 + 8 071

5. **(a)** 13 250 + 100 **(b)** 23 200 + 101
(c) 44 500 + 99 **(d)** 87 200 + 200
(e) 75 000 + 1 000 **(f)** 35 250 + 1 001
(g) 22 550 + 999 **(h)** 50 505 + 2 000

6. Write down the most important thing to think about when adding numbers in your head.

Addition short cuts

Work out a strategy to calculate the following in your heads. Explain your strategy in your book.

1. 3 + 7 + 3 + 7 + 3 + 7
2. 4 + 6 + 4 + 6 + 4 + 7
3. 2 + 18 + 2 + 18 + 2 + 18
4. 4 + 16 + 4 + 16 + 4 + 16 + 4 + 16 + 4 + 16
5. 5 + 95 + 5 + 95 + 5 + 95
6. 40 + 60 + 30 + 70 + 20 + 80
7. 7 + 93 + 81
8. 4 + 73 + 96
9. 1 + 2 + 3 + 4 + 5 + 6 + 7 +8 + 9
10. 1 + 9 + 2 + 8 + 3 + 7 + 4 + 6 + 5 + 5
11. 3 + 17 + 3 + 17 + 3 + 17 + 3 + 18
12. 12 + 356 + 88
13. 200 + 800 + 300 + 700 + 150 + 850
14. 17 + 15 + 11 + 89 + 85 + 83
15. 49 + 51 + 48 + 52 + 47 + 53
16. 1 + 29 + 2 + 28 + 3 + 27
17. 1 + 2 + 3 + 4 + 999 + 998 + 997 + 996
18. 37 + 13 + 12 + 38
19. 101 + 99 + 101 + 99
20. 205 + 95 + 205 + 95
21. 99 + 99 + 99 + 99
22. 100 + 150 + 100 + 150 + 100 + 150

Addition

Write the following questions into your books, and add the numbers together. You could set them out like this.

$$\begin{array}{r} 2\ 5\ 7 \\ +\ {}_{1}3\ {}_{1}6\ 8 \\ \hline 6\ 2\ 5 \\ \hline \end{array}$$

1. **(a)** 327 + 159 **(b)** 286 + 416
   (c) 325 + 275 **(d)** 382 + 456
   (e) 571 + 393 **(f)** 466 + 282

2. **(a)** 1 376 + 217 **(b)** 3 418 + 255
   (c) 371 + 2 361 **(d)** 286 + 1 457
   (e) 3 827 + 625 **(f)** 5 286 + 396

3. **(a)** 2 061 + 1 077 **(b)** 3 284 + 4 327
   (c) 1 427 + 3 747 **(d)** 2 251 + 3 864
   (e) 3 872 + 4 786 **(f)** 8 020 + 1 893

4. **(a)** 12 381 + 24 776 **(b)** 24 784 + 32 889
   (c) 30 705 + 61 537 **(d)** 35 981 + 6 752
   (e) 73 502 + 5 533 **(f)** 64 272 + 3 388

5. Write down the most important thing to think about when doing addition.

Finding the super answer

Copy into your book, and calculate the super answer.

1.

327	+	508	+	629	=	
+		+		+		+
869	+	236	+	247	=	
+		+		+		+
478	+	802	+	329	=	
	+		+		=	

2.

357	+	1 062	+	304	=	
+		+		+		+
816	+	7 071	+	291	=	
+		+		+		+
108	+	2 871	+	567	=	
	+		+		=	

3.

12 385	+	2 764	+	13 591	=	
+		+		+		+
20 040	+	4 871	+	56 002	=	
+		+		+		+
30 487	+	2 896	+	23 950	=	
	+		+		=	

4. Make up your own super problem that has a super answer of 5 000.

Different words for addition

Calculate the answers to the following questions.

1. What is 15 more than 37?

2. What is 327 added to 281?

3. What is 423 plus 388?

4. What is the total of 837, 1 028, and 357?

5. So far today I have travelled 27 km. I still have 34 km to travel. How far will I travel altogether?

6. There are 320 people at a football match. 570 more people arrive. How many people are there altogether?

7. This list shows the number of islands in some provinces in PNG.

Milne Bay	438 islands
Manus	208 islands
Bougainville	168 islands

   What is the total number of islands in these three provinces?

8. This list shows the size of some lakes in PNG.

Lake Kutubu	4 924 hectares
Lake Chambri	21 600 hectares
Lake Murray	64 700 hectares

   What is the size of these lakes altogether?

9. The following table shows some union membership figures.

PNG Teachers' Association	14 750
Police Association	4 800
Porgera Mining Workers' Union	2 250

   What is the total membership of these 3 unions?

Addition story problems with extra numbers

1. On Monday 346 people arrived on a Boeing 737, and on Thursday 355 people arrived. How many people arrived altogether?
2. There are 77 students in grade 3 and 68 students in grade 4. What is the total number of students in both grades?

3. A tin of coffee weighs 2 500 g and is 25 cm tall, and a tin of corn weighs 500 g and is 13 cm tall. What is the height of the tins if one is placed on top of the other? How heavy are the tins together?
4. The trip from Lae to Port Moresby takes 45 minutes and costs K223. The trip from Port Moresby to Daru takes 55 minutes and costs K285. There is usually a wait of 35 minutes in Port Moresby. How long should the trip from Lae to Daru via Port Moresby take?
5. In the first film night of the year there were 65 adults who paid K3 and 120 children who paid K2 each. On the second film night there were 82 adults, and 176 children. What is the total number of people who came to the films?
6. If a PMV has 15 seats, but has 22 passengers, and another PMV has 22 seats and 33 passengers, how many passengers are there altogether?

Adding distances

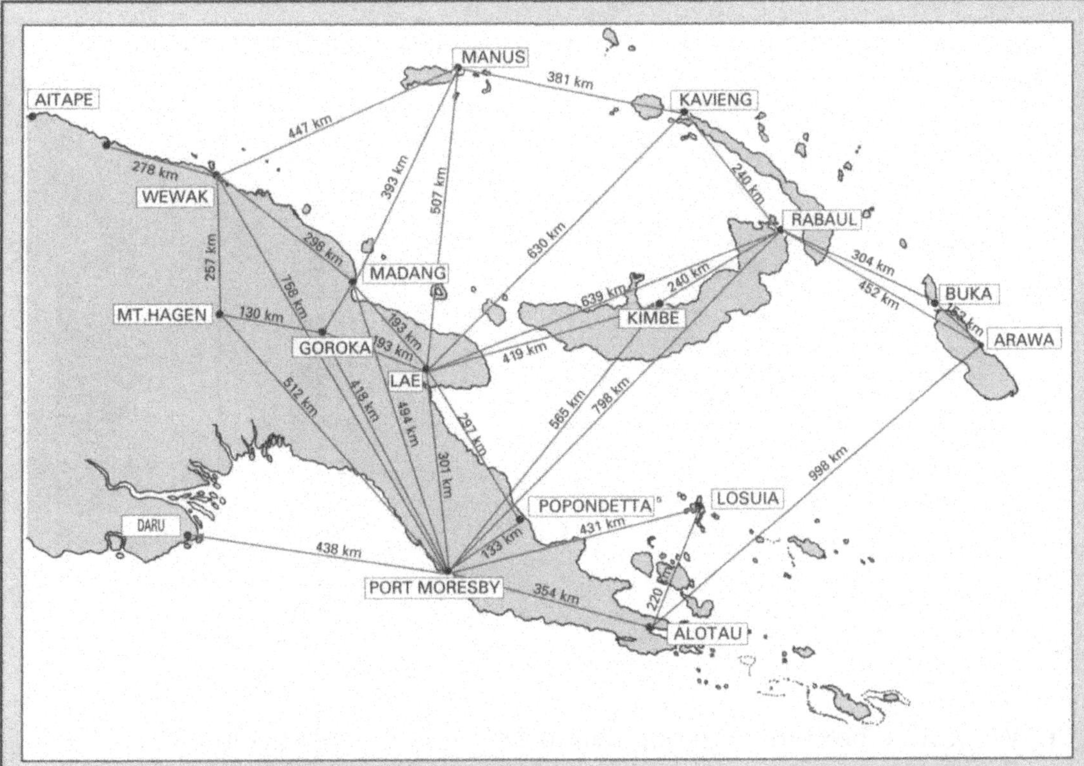

Answer these questions in your books.

1. What is the distance to travel from Aitape to Lae via Wewak and Madang?
2. What is the distance from Kavieng to Port Moresby via Lae?
3. What is the distance from Rabaul to Port Moresby via Lae?
4. Which place is furthest from Port Moresby: Arawa, Rabaul or Kavieng?
5. What is the distance from Port Moresby to Losuia via Alotau?
6. What is the distance from Aitape to Arawa via Wewak, Madang, Lae, and Rabaul?
7. I went on a trip that was 585 km. Where did I travel?
8. I went on a trip that was longer than 600 km but less than 700 km. Where might I have travelled? (There may be more than 1 answer.)

Population of provinces

This table shows the population of the provinces in PNG as it was in the Year 2000.

Province	2 000
Bougainville	189 574
Central	171 692
East New Britain	260 064
East Sepik	291 672
Eastern Highlands	326 482
Enga	338 287
Gulf	72 840
Madang	304 684
Manus	41 469
Milne Bay	197 013
Morobe	469 592
National Capital	315 244
New Ireland	114 329
Oro	120 910
Sandaun	169 454
Simbu	189 233
Southern Highlands	430 158
West New Britain	191 934
Western	137 815
Western Highlands	429 586

1. What was the combined population of Central Province and East New Britain Province?
2. How many people lived in Enga and Gulf combined?
3. What was the combined population of the two provinces with the highest populations?
4. What was the combined population of the three provinces with the lowest populations?
5. How many people lived in the Highlands Region?
6. What was the total population of all the islands?
7. Someone added 260 064 + 191 934. What do you think they were trying to work out?
8. The answer is 210 655. What is the question? How did you work it out?
9. I have a friend who is from a province that has a population larger than Bougainville but smaller than Milne Bay. Where do you think my friend is from?

Classifying triangles

Find all the:

1. scalene triangles
2. isosceles triangles
3. equilateral triangles
4. triangles that have only acute angles
5. triangles that have one obtuse angle
6. right-angled triangles

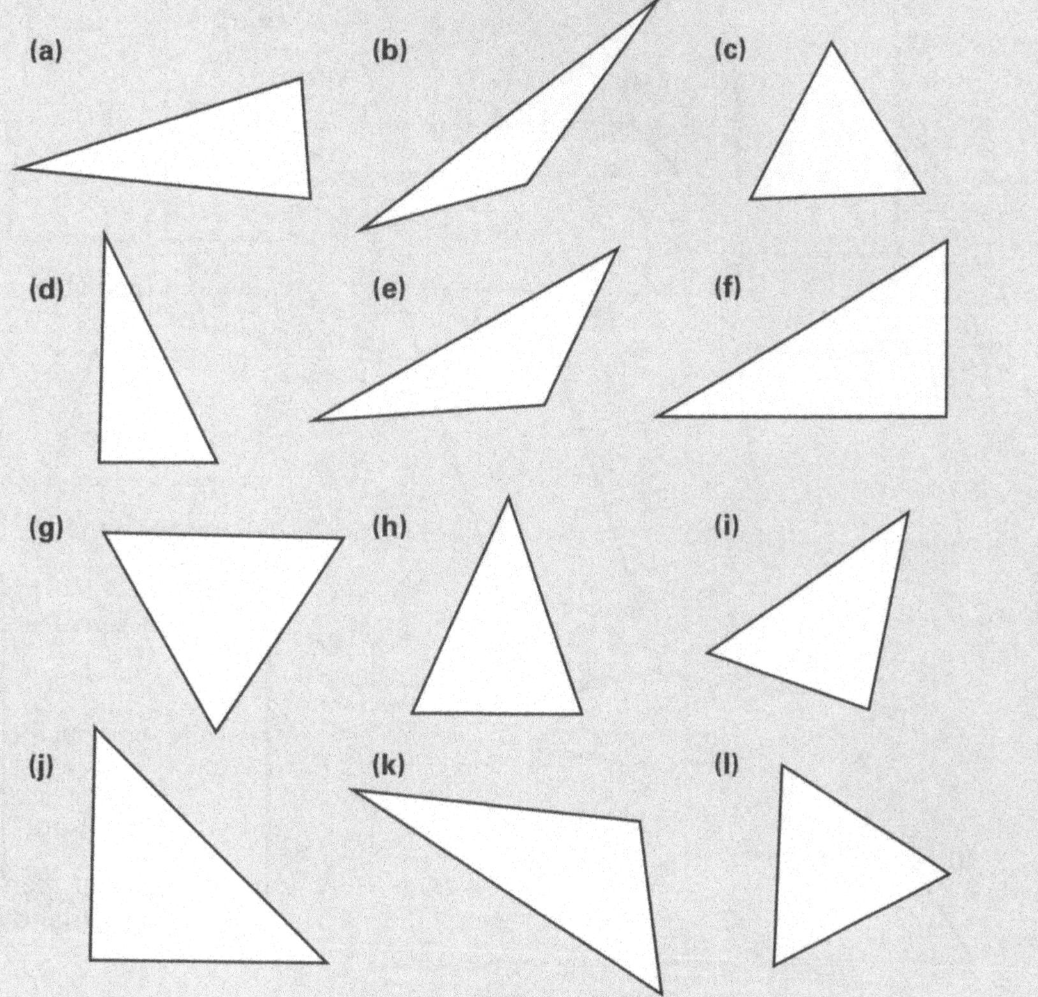

Comparing parallelograms and trapeziums

Which shapes are parallelograms?

Which shapes are trapeziums?

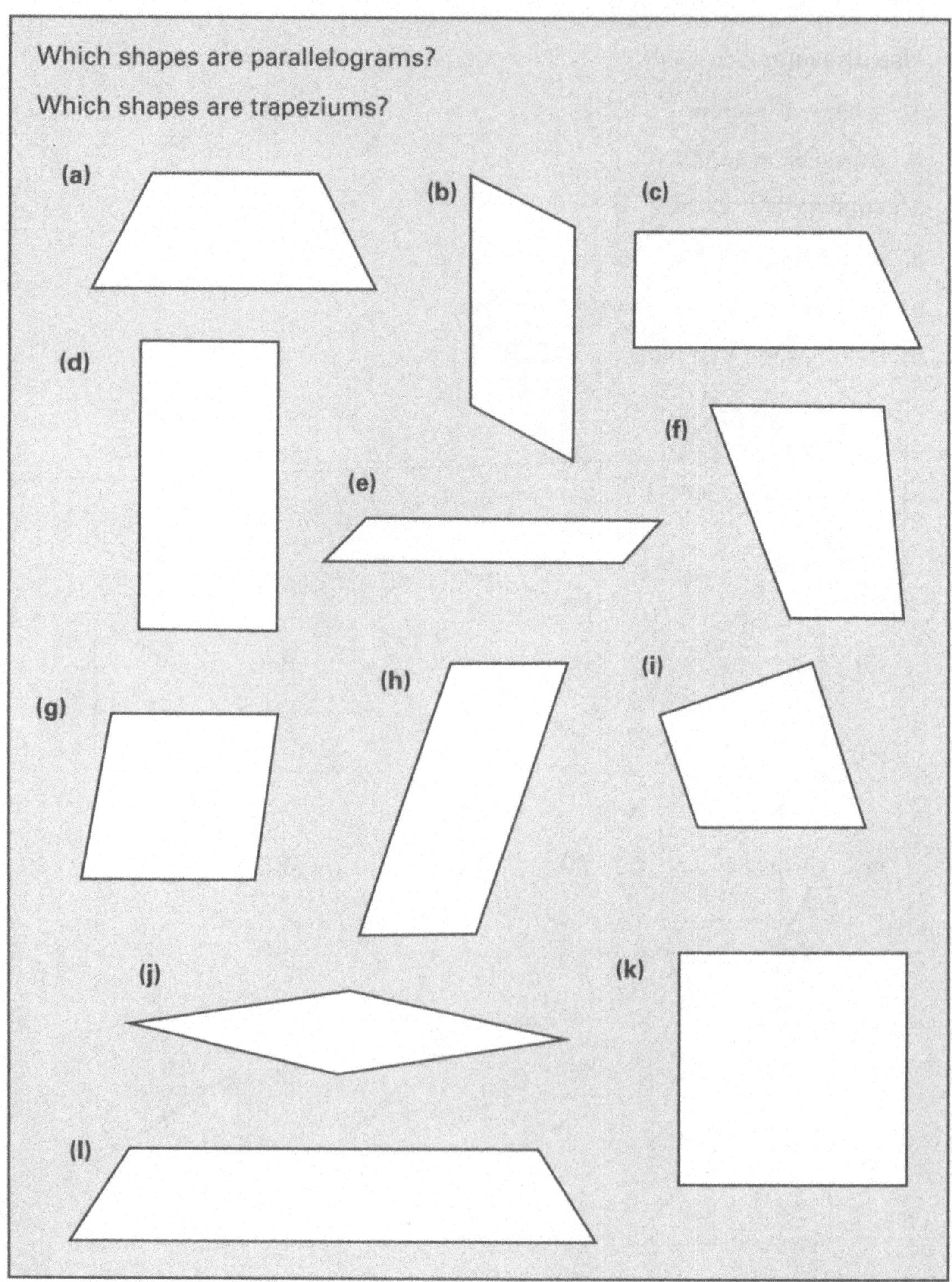

Tangram puzzles

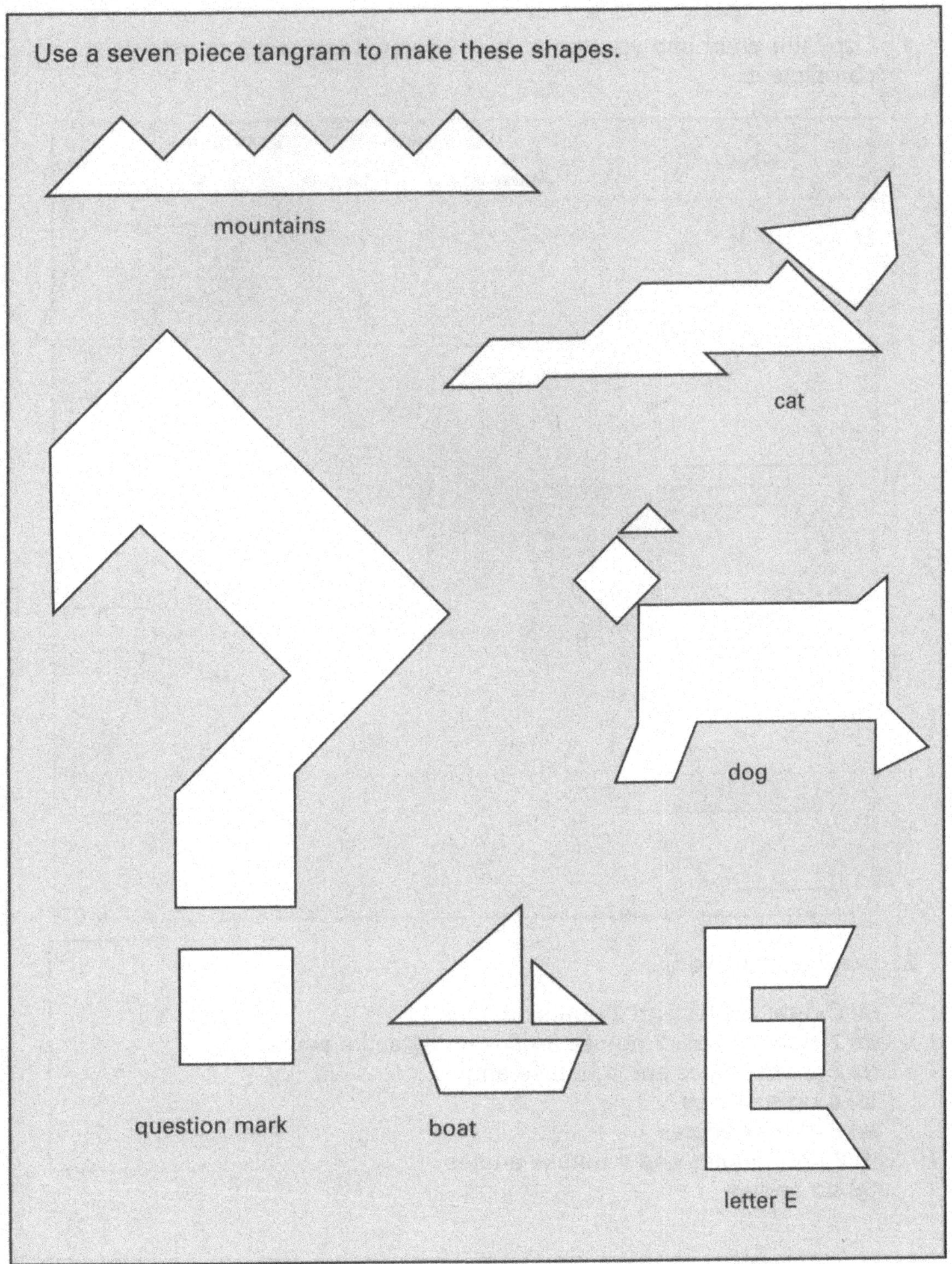

Finding and classifying angles

1. Copy this chart into your book, then use an angle tester to help you complete it.

Shape	Number of each type of angle		
	Acute	Obtuse	Right

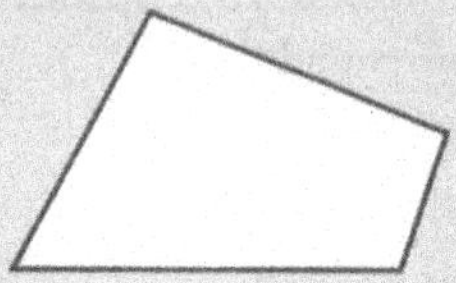			
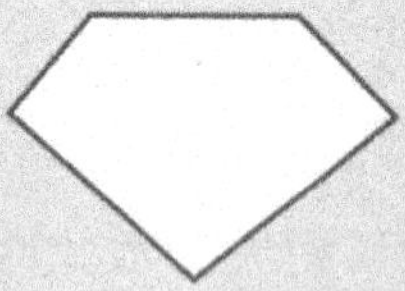			

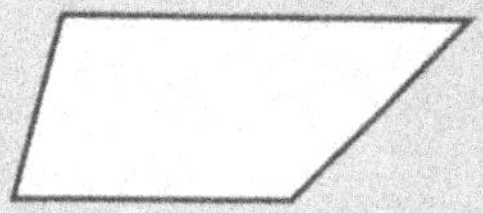			

2. Draw a shape with:

   (a) 2 right angles and 2 obtuse angles
   (b) 2 right angles, 2 obtuse angles and 1 acute angle
   (c) 2 acute angles and 4 obtuse angles
   (d) 4 right angles
   (e) 8 obtuse angles
   (f) 2 right angles and 4 obtuse angles
   (g) no angles

Folding circles to make shapes

Use compasses to draw 5 large circles. Fold each circle as shown, then open and rule the shape with a pencil.

1.

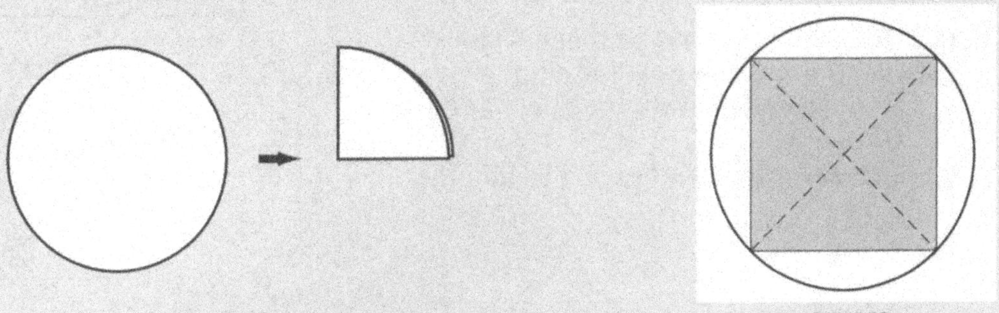

square

2.

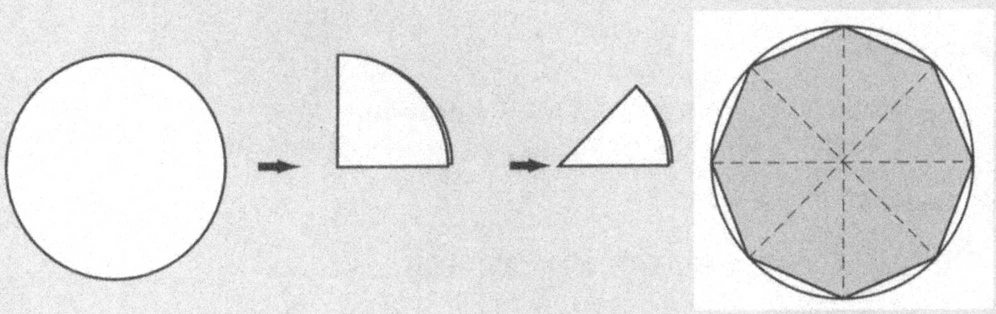

octagon

3.

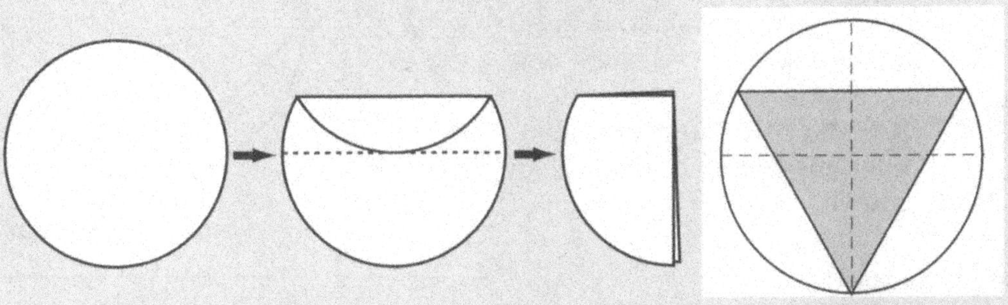

triangle

4.

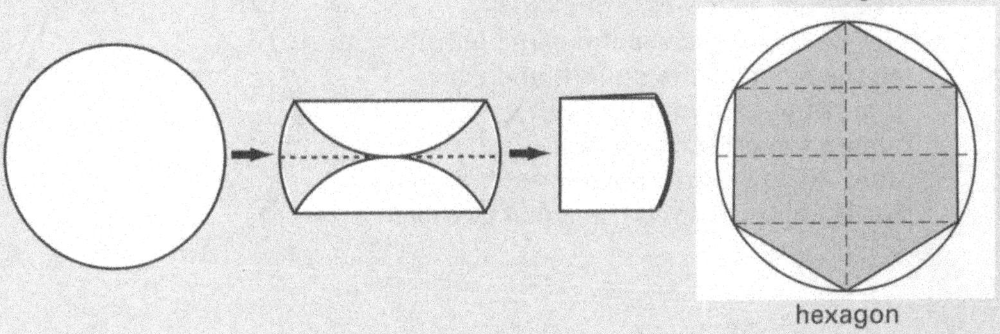

hexagon

Using a compass to help construct shapes

Use compasses and a ruler to construct these shapes inside a circle.

1. Hexagon

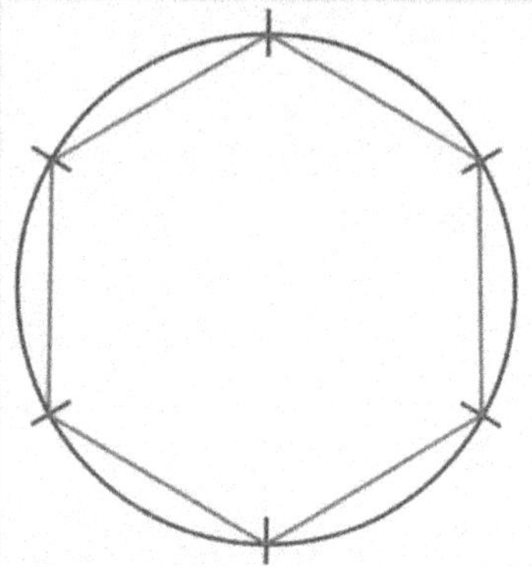

(a) Use your compass to make a circle.
(b) Using the same position on the compass place it on the circle and mark around it.
(c) Use your ruler and pencil to join the marks.

2. Triangle

(a) Make marks like you did for the hexagon.
(b) Use your ruler and pencil to join every second mark.

3. Square

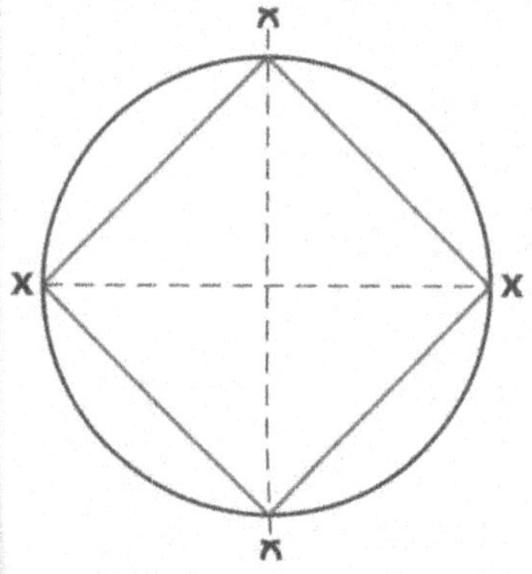

(a) Make a circle and rule a line through the centre.
(b) Open your compasses the diameter of the circle and make marks by placing it on each side of the circle where the crosses are (x).
(c) Join the two marks and then use your ruler and pencil to draw a square as shown.

4. Octagon

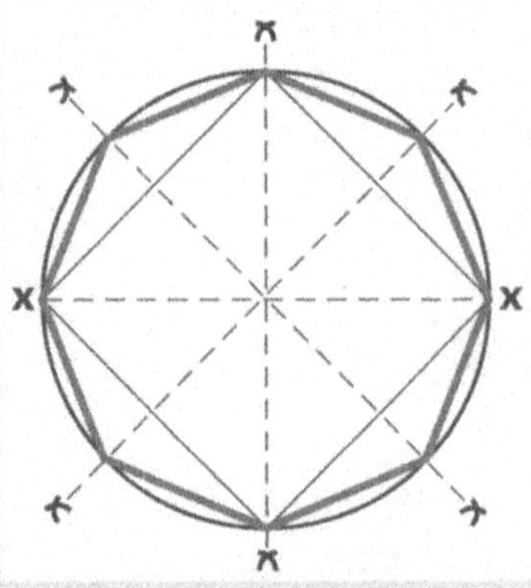

(a) Construct a square in the circle.
(b) Set your compasses the same length as the sides of the square and make marks by placing it on each corner where the crosses are (x).
(c) Join the opposite marks and then join the 8 points around the circle to make an octagon.

Subtraction your way

Copy the questions into your book and write the answer as a number sentence (**do the calculation in your head**).
e.g. 220 – 100 = 120

1. **(a)** 324 – 100 **(b)** 476 – 100
(c) 245 – 99 **(d)** 709 – 99
(e) 1 279 – 100 **(f)** 1 386 – 100
(g) 2 417 – 99 **(h)** 3 529 – 99

2. **(a)** 476 – 20 **(b)** 327 – 20
(c) 477 – 50 **(d)** 382 – 50
(e) 1 277 – 20 **(f)** 8 251 – 20
(g) 3 040 – 50 **(h)** 2 197 – 50

3. **(a)** 872 – 101 **(b)** 426 – 101
(c) 262 – 101 **(d)** 357 – 101
(e) 283 – 200 **(f)** 631 – 200
(g) 535 – 200 **(h)** 901 – 200

4. **(a)** 387 – 251 **(b)** 894 – 461
(c) 973 – 316 **(d)** 2 468 – 307
(e) 2 538 – 1 525 **(f)** 8 279 – 1 006
(g) 6 659 – 1 327 **(h)** 5 387 – 4 071

5. **(a)** 13 250 – 100 **(b)** 23 200 – 101
(c) 44 500 – 99 **(d)** 87 200 - 200
(e) 75 000 – 1 000 **(f)** 35 250 – 1 001
(g) 22 550 – 999 **(h)** 50 505 – 2 000

6. **(a)** 876 – 100 – 99 **(b)** 638 – 100 – 99
(c) 291 – 100 – 99 **(d)** 405 – 100 – 99
(e) 5 922 – 100 – 99 **(f)** 3 968 – 100 – 99
(g) 1 900 – 100 – 99 **(h)** 5 000 – 100 – 99

7. Write down the most important thing to think about when subtracting numbers in your head.

Making it up to …

Copy the questions into your book and write the answer as a number sentence (**do the calculation in your head**).
e.g. 1 000 – 330 = 670

1. **(a)** 100 – 34 **(b)** 100 – 65
(c) 100 – 82 **(d)** 100 – 49
(e) 100 – 71 **(f)** 200 – 32
(g) 500 – 120 **(h)** 700 – 185

2. **(a)** 1 000 – 350 **(b)** 1 000 – 222
(c) 1 000 – 780 **(d)** 1 000 – 987
(e) 1 000 – 880 **(f)** 1 000 – 320
(g) 1 000 – 235 **(h)** 1 000 – 655

3. **(a)** 2 000 – 150 **(b)** 2 000 – 1 450
(c) 2 000 – 85 **(d)** 2 000 – 1 880
(e) 3 000 – 1 400 **(f)** 3 000 – 150
(g) 5 000 – 2 222 **(h)** 8 000 – 2 500

4. **(a)** 10 000 – 3 000 **(b)** 10 000 – 2 500
(c) 10 000 – 3 200 **(d)** 10 000 – 6 800
(e) 10 000 – 2 200 **(f)** 10 000 – 675
(g) 10 000 – 32 **(h)** 10 000 – 1 234

5. **(a)** 20 000 – 1 500 **(b)** 20 000 – 16 500
(c) 20 000 – 850 **(d)** 20 000 – 1 234
(e) 70 000 – 25 000 **(f)** 40 000 – 650
(g) 80 000 – 32 000 **(h)** 90 000 – 65 500

6. Write down the most important thing to think about when making numbers up to 100, 1 000 or 10 000 in your head.

Subtraction

Write the following questions into your books, and subtract the smaller number from the larger one. You could set them out like this:

$$\begin{array}{r} {}^{7}\not{8}\,{}^{1}2\;\;7 \\ -\;3\;\;7\;\;1 \\ \hline 4\;\;5\;\;6 \\ \hline \end{array}$$

1. (a) 387 – 159 (b) 786 – 418
   (c) 483 – 356 (d) 823 – 166
   (e) 472 – 195 (f) 507 – 144

2. (a) 1 872 – 338 (b) 3 418 – 815
   (c) 2 905 – 672 (d) 2 453 – 967
   (e) 2 005 – 384 (f) 8 012 – 405
   (g) 9 256 – 782 (h) 3 006 – 390

3. (a) 5 683 – 1 027 (b) 3 284 – 1 922
   (c) 5 038 – 1 522 (d) 7 505 – 2 388
   (e) 7 440 – 2 824 (f) 3 003 – 678
   (g) 5 087 – 3 105 (h) 8 391 – 5 989

4. (a) 52 381 – 24 716 (b) 24 784 – 15 389
   (c) 30 705 – 1 537 (d) 35 981 – 16 752
   (e) 73 002 – 25 533 (f) 64 000 – 43 388
   (g) 78 500 – 24 995 (h) 90 005 – 32 457

5. (a) 36 201 – 157 (b) 45 902 – 388
   (c) 26 156 – 519 (d) 45 002 – 2 177
   (e) 86 070 – 3 509 (f) 35 000 –1 256

6. Write down the most important thing to think about when answering subtraction questions.

Different words for subtraction

Calculate the answers to the following questions.

1. What is 238 less than 677?
2. What is 327 take away 281?
3. What is 4 023 minus 3 808?
4. 1 008 is 405 more than what number?
5. In an athletics competition, Tau scored 3 050 points and Raku scored 2 468 points. What is the difference between their scores?
6. There are 3 320 people at a football match. After 570 people leave, how many people are still there?
7. This list shows the number of speakers of some of the language groups in PNG.

Huli	60 883 speakers
Simbu	137 654 speakers
Abelam	33 100 speakers
Kewa	48 121 speakers

(a) How many more people speak Huli than Kewa?
(b) How many more people speak Simbu than Abelam?
(c) What is the difference between the number of Huli speakers and the number of Simbu speakers?

8. This list shows the number of workers in various industries in PNG.

Agriculture	35 795 workers
Trade	25 645 workers
Manufacturing	13 023 workers
Construction	12 313 workers

(a) How many more workers are there in Agriculture than in Trade?
(b) How many less workers are there in Construction than in Manufacturing?
(c) What is the difference between the number of workers in Construction and Agriculture?

Subtraction story problems

1. On Monday 21st February, 1 130 people arrived in Port Moresby by plane, and on Thursday 24th February, 807 people arrived. How many more people arrived on Monday 21st?

2. In PNG in 1995 there were 4 798 new trucks and a total of 27 480 registered. How many trucks were there that were more than one year old?

3. In a school there are 68 students who are 10 years old and 106 who are 11 years old. How many more 11 year olds are there than 10 year olds?

4. How much higher is Mt Wilhelm at 4 509 metres than Mt Bedego at 3 774 metres?

5. In the first film night of the year there were 65 adults who paid K3 and 120 children who paid K2 each. On the second film night there were 82 adults, and 176 children. How many more children were there altogether than there were adults altogether?

6. From 1972 to 1992, the Bougainville mine produced 3 100 000 tonnes of copper. Ok Tedi has produced 999 175 tonnes of copper since it started in 1984. How much more copper was produced in Bougainville than in Ok Tedi?

7. Eleven boys play Under 14 soccer and five boys play Under 15 basketball. How many more boys play soccer than basketball?

8. Fifteen passengers were in a double cab Hilux and seven were in a single cab Hilux. How many more passengers were there in the double cab Hilux?

9. A galip tree with 300 fruit grew to 18 metres. A banana tree with 30 fruit grew to 2 metres. How much taller was the galip tree than the banana tree?

Ship visits

The following information refers to the total number of ship visits to some PNG ports and to the amount of overseas cargo carried.

Port	Ship Visits	Overseas Cargo (tonnes)
Port Moresby	761	416 237
Lae	1 378	447 619
Rabaul	1 148	768 619
Kiunga/Daru	167	447 439
Madang	640	219 839

1. How much more overseas cargo is carried through Lae than through Port Moresby?
2. What is the difference between the number of ship visits to Rabaul and Madang?
3. How many fewer ship visits are made at Daru than at Port Moresby?
4. The port of Kimbe has more ship visits than Daru but less than Madang. How many visits do you think there might be in Kimbe?
5. Which two ports have the smallest difference between the number of ship calls?
6. Which two ports have the largest difference between the amount of cargo carried?

7. ✎ Challenge activity ✎

I worked out a question using the table at the top of the page. The answer was 473. What was the question?

Bar graph titles

A

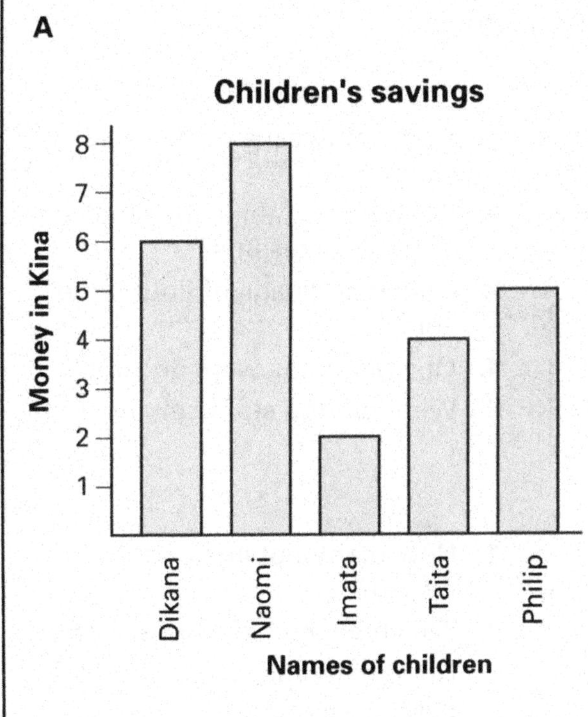

1. Who has saved the most money?
2. How much have they saved in total?
3. How much more has Taita saved than Imata?
4. How much less has Philip saved than Naomi?
5. How much have Dikana and Philip saved between them?
6. How many more kina does Imata need to have K10?

B

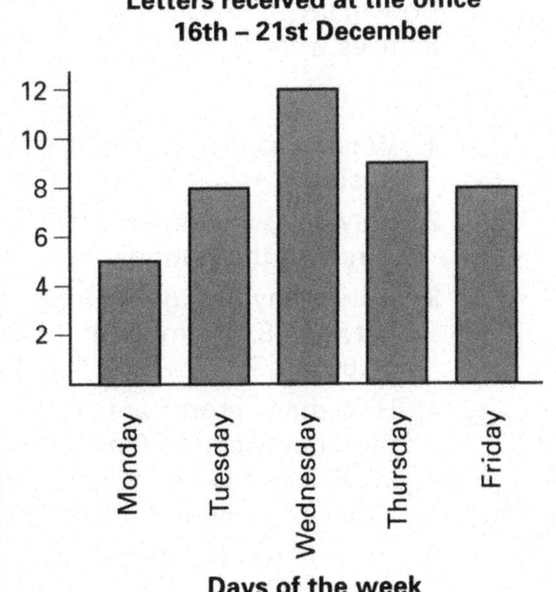

1. Write a label for the vertical axis.
2. How many letters arrived in the office during this week?
3. On which days did an odd number of letters arrive?
4. On which days did eight letters arrive?
5. How many letters arrived on Friday?
6. What type of letters could there have been? How do you know this?

Reading picture graphs

Answer the questions about each picture graph.

A

Trade store sales for 1 month	
Tins of tuna	
Cans of drink	
Bags of flour	
Tins of coffee	
Bags of rice	
Each picture represents 10 sales	

1. How many cans of drink were sold?
2. What do you think the small can of tuna represents?
3. How many bags of flour were sold?
4. Of what items were 30 sold?
5. What did the store sell most of?

B

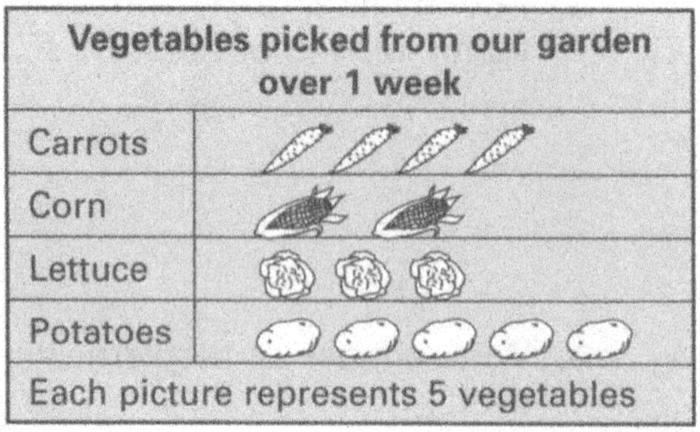

Vegetables picked from our garden over 1 week	
Carrots	
Corn	
Lettuce	
Potatoes	
Each picture represents 5 vegetables	

1. How many potatoes were picked?
2. Which vegetables had 20 picked?
3. How many more lettuces than corn were picked?
4. How many vegetables were picked altogether?
5. How many more carrots than lettuces were picked?

C

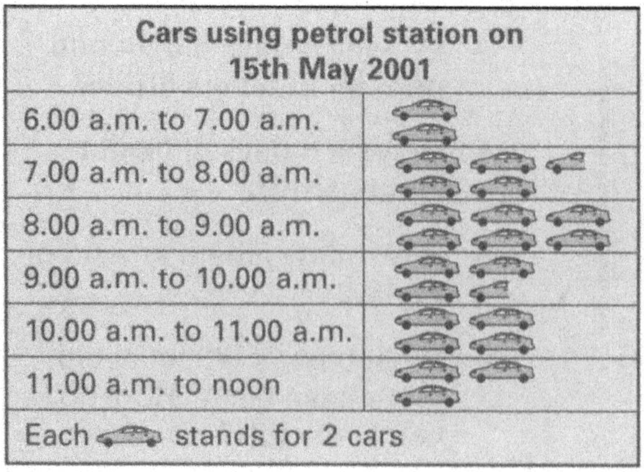

Cars using petrol station on 15th May 2001	
6.00 a.m. to 7.00 a.m.	
7.00 a.m. to 8.00 a.m.	
8.00 a.m. to 9.00 a.m.	
9.00 a.m. to 10.00 a.m.	
10.00 a.m. to 11.00 a.m.	
11.00 a.m. to noon	
Each [car] stands for 2 cars	

1. When was the petrol station busiest?
2. Between what times did 9 cars visit the station?
3. How many cars got petrol between 8.00 a.m. and 10.00 a.m.?
4. How many more cars got petrol between 9.00 a.m. and 10.00 a.m. than between 11.00 a.m. and noon?
5. How many cars visited the station?

Reading circle graphs

Answer the questions about each circle graph.

A

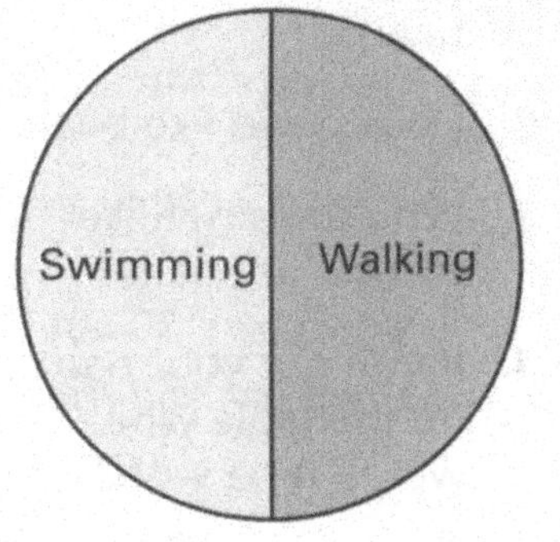

1. If 200 people were surveyed how many preferred swimming?
2. What fraction of people chose walking?
3. Ask 5 classmates what they would prefer to do.

B

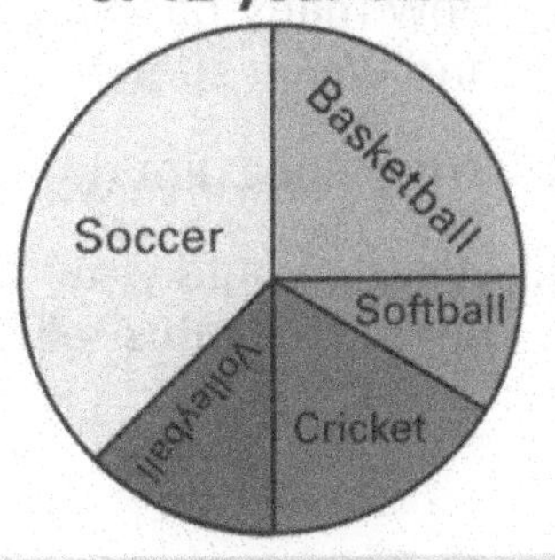

1. What game do most children choose?
2. What is the least favourite game?
3. If 100 children were surveyed, about how many chose basketball?

C

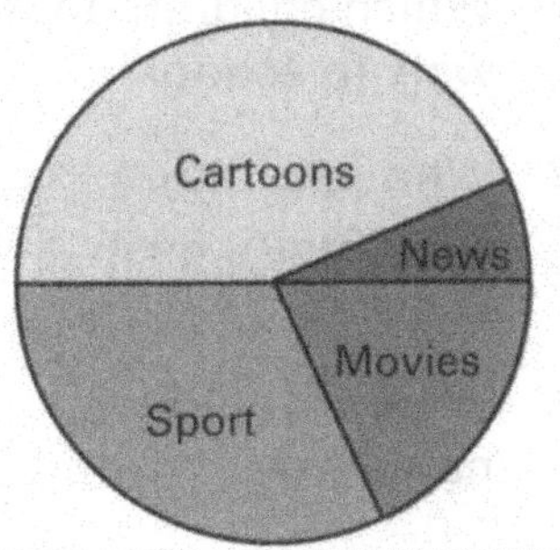

1. What is the most popular programme?
2. Approximately what fraction of children watch movies?
3. If 100 children were surveyed, about how many chose each program?

Interpreting two-way tables

Use the two-way table to help answer the questions.

A

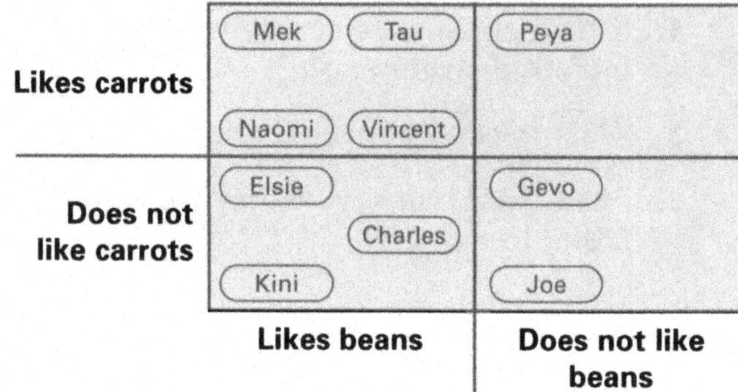

1. Name two children who like carrots and beans.
2. Does Gevo like beans?
3. Who does not like carrots or beans?
4. If you put your name on the table who would it be with?

B

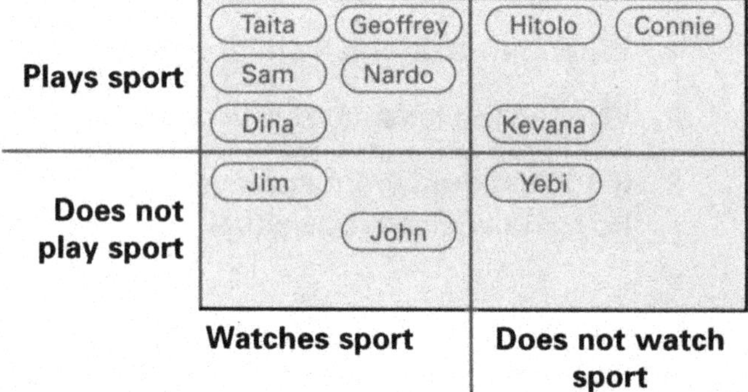

1. Who does not play or watch sport?
2. How many people play and watch sport?
3. What does Jim do?
4. Where would your name fit on this table?

C

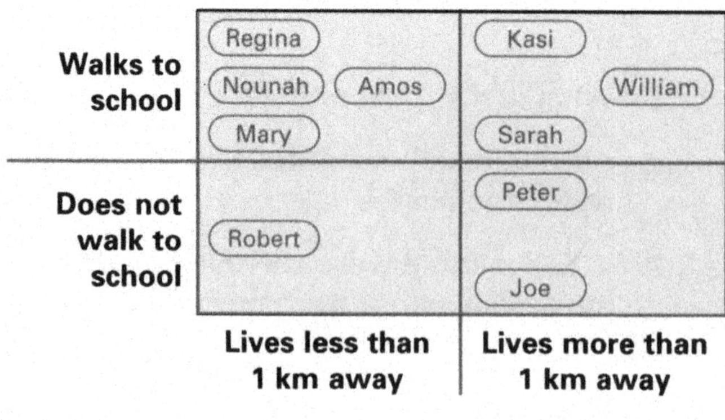

1. How many children live more than 1 kilometre from school?
2. Which children do not walk to school?
3. Who lives more than 1 kilometre away and walks to school?
4. Where would your name fit?

Interpreting other tables

Use each table to answer the questions next to it.

A

New vehicle registration

Trucks	4 798
Cars, station wagons	1 847
Buses	463
Tractors	286
Motorcycles	371

1. How many vehicles were registered altogether?
2. How many more buses were registered than tractors?
3. What type of vehicle had the most registrations?

B

Temperature in degrees Celsius for different altitudes

Altitude (metres)	Highest temperature	Lowest temperature
Sea level	32	23
600	30	19
1 200	27	16
1 800	23	12
2 100	21	11
2 400	19	9
2 800	16	7

1. What is the highest temperature for places 1 800 metres above sea level?
2. How cold does it get 2 800 metres above sea level?
3. Is it warmer 1 200 metres above sea level than at sea level?

C

Percentage of males/females who play sport

Age	Males	Females
0 to 14 years old	63%	58%
15 to 29 years old	75%	26%
30 to 45 years old	65%	10%
45 years and older	40%	8%

1. What percentage of females 45 years and older play sport?
2. What percentage of males 0 to 14 years old play sport?
3. In which age group do 75% of males play sport?

Fractions on number lines

Copy each of these number lines into your books. On as many lines as possible mark in the following: $1\frac{1}{2}$, $5\frac{1}{2}$, $\frac{3}{4}$, $2\frac{1}{4}$, $3\frac{1}{2}$

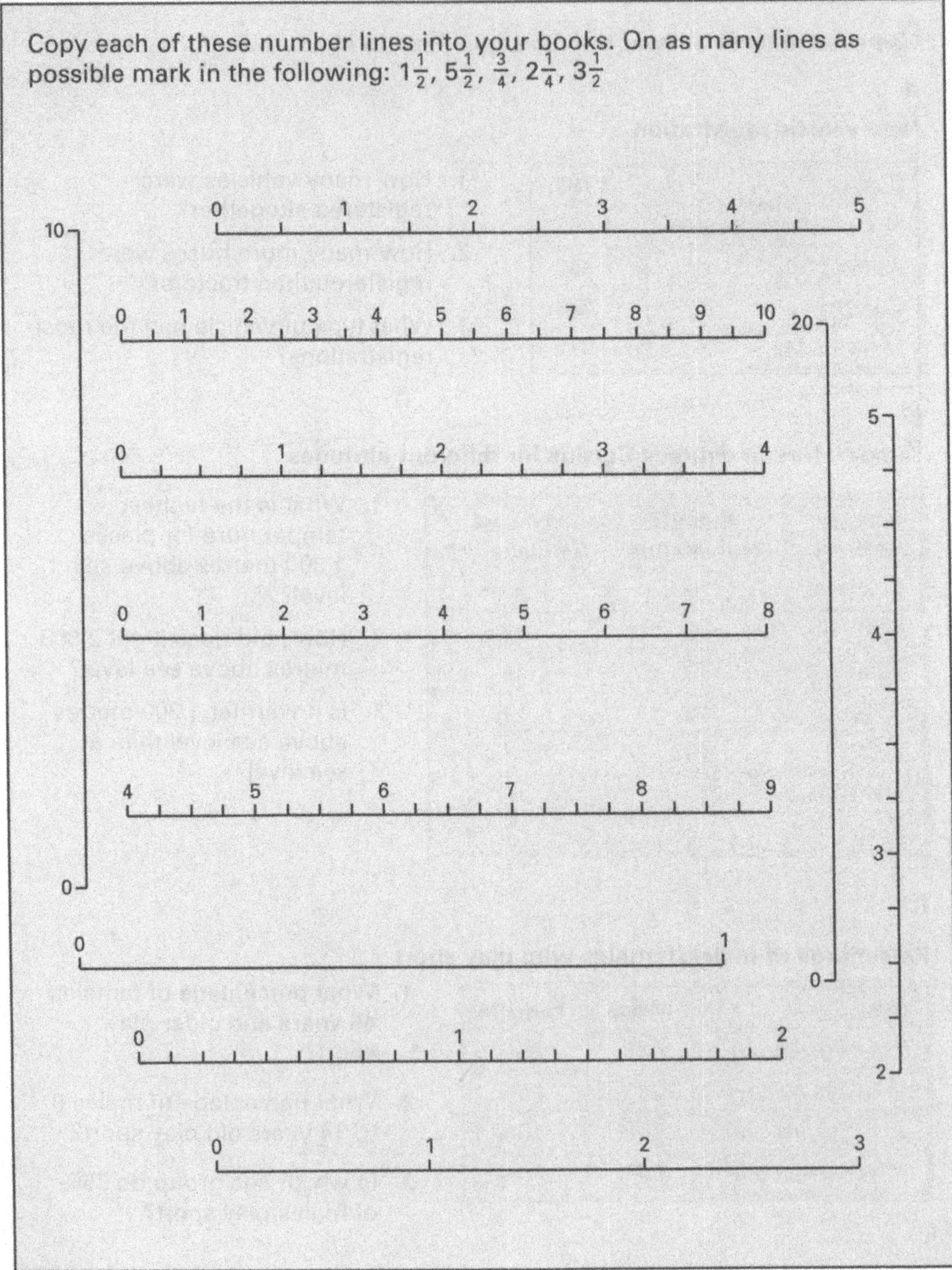

Fractions in different ways

Copy these tables into your books, and fill in the empty cells.

1.

Diagram	Number line	Part of groups	Symbol
	0 $\frac{1}{4}$ $\frac{1}{2}$ $\frac{3}{4}$ 1		
	0 $\frac{1}{4}$ $\frac{1}{2}$ $\frac{3}{4}$ 1		
	0 $\frac{1}{4}$ $\frac{1}{2}$ $\frac{3}{4}$ 1		
	0 $\frac{1}{4}$ $\frac{1}{2}$ $\frac{3}{4}$ 1		$\frac{1}{8}$

2. **Challenge activity**

Problem	Number line	Using words	Symbols
What fraction of a week is one day?	0 $\frac{1}{4}$ $\frac{1}{2}$ $\frac{3}{4}$ 1		
What fraction of a soccer team is the goalkeeper?	0 $\frac{1}{4}$ $\frac{1}{2}$ $\frac{3}{4}$ 1		
What fraction of your class are girls?	0 $\frac{1}{4}$ $\frac{1}{2}$ $\frac{3}{4}$ 1		
What fraction of the letters on this page are vowels?	0 $\frac{1}{4}$ $\frac{1}{2}$ $\frac{3}{4}$ 1		
	0 $\frac{1}{4}$ $\frac{1}{2}$ $\frac{3}{4}$ 1		$\frac{3}{10}$
What fraction of the provinces in PNG are in the Highlands?	0 $\frac{1}{4}$ $\frac{1}{2}$ $\frac{3}{4}$ 1		

Fraction patterns

Copy the following fraction patterns into your books and complete the missing numbers.

1. $\frac{1}{2}$, 1, $1\frac{1}{2}$, 2, ___, ___, ___, ___, ___, ___

2. 5, $5\frac{1}{4}$, $5\frac{2}{4}$, $5\frac{3}{4}$, 6, $6\frac{1}{4}$, ___, ___, ___, ___, ___, ___

3. $\frac{5}{10}$, $\frac{6}{10}$, $\frac{7}{10}$, $\frac{8}{10}$, ___, ___, ___, ___, ___, ___

4. 10, $9\frac{1}{2}$, ___, ___, ___, ___, ___, ___, 6, $5\frac{1}{2}$

5. $7\frac{1}{5}$, $7\frac{2}{5}$, $7\frac{3}{5}$, $7\frac{4}{5}$, ___, ___, ___, ___, ___, ___

6. $3\frac{1}{3}$, $3\frac{2}{3}$, 4, $4\frac{1}{3}$, $4\frac{2}{3}$, ___, ___, ___, ___, ___, ___

7. $\frac{3}{4}$, $1\frac{1}{4}$, ___, ___, ___, ___, ___, ___, $4\frac{3}{4}$, $5\frac{1}{4}$

8. $12\frac{1}{2}$, $11\frac{1}{2}$, $10\frac{1}{2}$, $9\frac{1}{2}$, ___, ___, ___, ___, ___, ___

9. 120, $120\frac{1}{4}$, $120\frac{2}{4}$, $120\frac{3}{4}$, ___, ___, ___, ___, ___, ___

10. $30\frac{7}{10}$, $30\frac{6}{10}$, $30\frac{5}{10}$, $30\frac{4}{10}$, ___, ___, ___, ___, ___, ___

11. 10, $11\frac{1}{2}$, 13, $14\frac{1}{2}$, 16, ___, ___, ___, ___, ___, ___

12. 32, 16, 8, 4, ___, ___, ___, ___, ___, ___

Equivalent fractions with numbers

Copy these questions into your books, and write in the missing number.

1. **(a)** $\frac{3}{5} = \frac{\square}{10}$ **(b)** $\frac{3}{4} = \frac{\square}{8}$ **(c)** $\frac{2}{3} = \frac{\square}{6}$

(d) $\frac{2}{3} = \frac{\square}{12}$ **(e)** $\frac{1}{5} = \frac{\square}{20}$ **(f)** $\frac{1}{4} = \frac{\square}{12}$

(g) $\frac{1}{3} = \frac{\square}{9}$ **(h)** $\frac{1}{3} = \frac{\square}{30}$

2. **(a)** $\frac{\square}{5} = \frac{8}{10}$ **(b)** $\frac{\square}{4} = \frac{4}{8}$ **(c)** $\frac{\square}{3} = \frac{4}{6}$

(d) $\frac{\square}{3} = \frac{8}{12}$ **(e)** $\frac{\square}{5} = \frac{12}{20}$ **(f)** $\frac{\square}{4} = \frac{6}{12}$

(g) $\frac{\square}{3} = \frac{3}{9}$ **(h)** $\frac{\square}{3} = \frac{10}{30}$

3. **(a)** $\frac{3}{5} = \frac{\square}{50}$ **(b)** $\frac{3}{4} = \frac{\square}{80}$ **(c)** $\frac{2}{3} = \frac{\square}{60}$

(d) $\frac{2}{3} = \frac{\square}{36}$ **(e)** $\frac{1}{5} = \frac{\square}{200}$ **(f)** $\frac{1}{4} = \frac{\square}{1\,000}$

(g) $\frac{1}{3} = \frac{\square}{900}$ **(h)** $\frac{1}{3} = \frac{\square}{3\,000}$

4. **(a)** $\frac{\square}{5} = \frac{80}{100}$ **(b)** $\frac{\square}{4} = \frac{10}{40}$ **(c)** $\frac{\square}{3} = \frac{21}{30}$

(d) $\frac{\square}{3} = \frac{60}{90}$ **(e)** $\frac{\square}{50} = \frac{80}{100}$ **(f)** $\frac{\square}{100} = \frac{100}{500}$

(g) $\frac{\square}{10} = \frac{10}{100}$ **(h)** $\frac{\square}{10} = \frac{40}{100}$

5. Write down as many fractions equivalent to $\frac{1}{2}$ as you can.

Fraction wall

Copy this fraction wall into your books.

The top row has a value of 1.

Each rectangle in the next row has a value of $\frac{1}{2}$. Write $\frac{1}{2}$ in each of the rectangles on the second row.

Each rectangle in the next row has a value of $\frac{1}{3}$. Write $\frac{1}{3}$ in each of the rectangles in the third row.

Write their value in each of the other rectangles.

By examining the wall, you can work out what fractions are the same. For example, $\frac{4}{8}$ is the same as $\frac{1}{2}$. Write this as $\frac{4}{8} = \frac{1}{2}$. These are called **equivalent fractions.**

1. What fractions are equivalent to $\frac{1}{2}$?
2. What fraction is equivalent to $\frac{1}{3}$?
3. What fraction is equivalent to $\frac{1}{4}$?
4. What fraction is equivalent to $\frac{3}{4}$?
5. What fraction is equivalent to $\frac{2}{3}$?

Fractions to decimals

1. Write the fractions indicated as decimals.

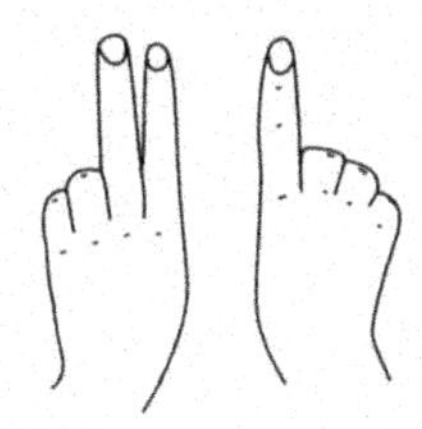
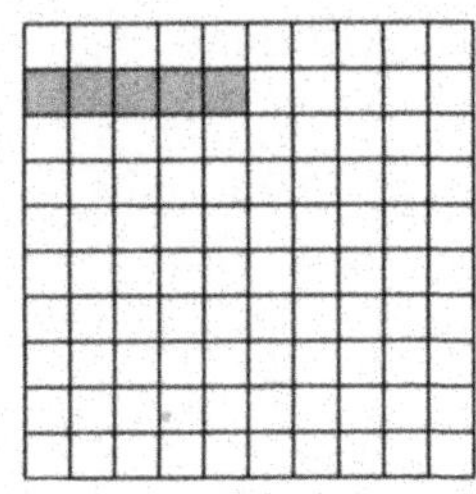
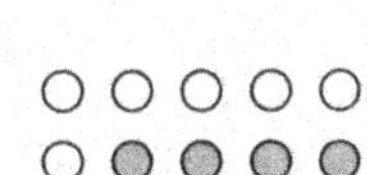
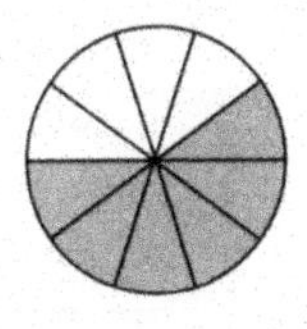

2. Write these fractions as decimals

(a) $\frac{1}{10}$ (b) $\frac{3}{10}$ (c) $\frac{25}{100}$

(d) $\frac{30}{100}$ (e) $\frac{78}{100}$ (f) $\frac{4}{10}$

(g) $\frac{3}{100}$ (h) $\frac{20}{100}$

3. Write the fractions indicated as a decimal.

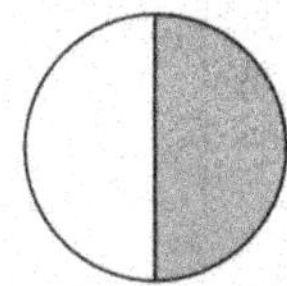
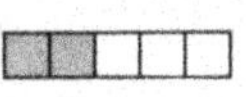

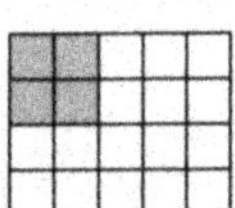

4. Write these fractions as decimals.

(a) $\frac{1}{5}$ (b) $\frac{1}{2}$ (c) $\frac{3}{5}$ (d) $\frac{2}{5}$

(e) $\frac{37}{50}$ (f) $\frac{41}{50}$ (g) $\frac{7}{50}$ (h) $\frac{24}{100}$

(i) $\frac{1}{20}$ (j) $\frac{11}{20}$ (k) $\frac{19}{20}$ (l) $\frac{15}{20}$

5. What is the most important thing to think about when changing fractions to decimals?

Decimals in different ways

Copy these tables into your books, and fill in the spaces.

1.

Diagram	Number line	Fraction	Decimal
	0 0.25 0.5 0.75 1		
	0 0.25 0.5 0.75 1		
	0 0.25 0.5 0.75 1	$\frac{1}{5}$	
	0 0.25 0.5 0.75 1		0.25

2.

Number line	Words	Decimal
0 1		
0 1	zero point four	
0 1		0.7

3.

Words	Symbols	Money
One kina and twenty toea		
	K1.50	

Numbers between

1. Write down a number between:

(a) 3.2 and 3.5
(b) 4.1 and 4.6
(c) 8.4 and 8.6
(d) 0.7 and 0.9
(e) 23.2 and 23.5
(f) 50.0 and 50.5
(g) 82.3 and 82.7
(h) 11.1 and 12.1

2. Write down a number between:

(a) 3.84 and 3.87
(b) 5.12 and 5.15
(c) 0.92 and 0.94
(d) 8.67 and 8.69
(e) 43.25 and 43.35
(f) 92.15 and 92.18
(g) 26.25 and 26.28
(h) 20.35 and 20.38

3. Write down a number between:

(a) 3.8 and 4
(b) 4 and 4.2
(c) 5 and 5.3
(d) 3.8 and 5
(e) 24.8 and 25
(f) 54 and 54.5
(g) 60 and 60.2
(h) 79.5 and 80

4. Write down a number between:

(a) 3.2 and 3.3
(b) 4.5 and 4.6
(c) 9.8 and 9.9
(d) 5.8 and 5.9
(e) 22.7 and 22.8
(f) 40.2 and 40.3
(g) 39.5 and 39.6
(h) 82.8 and 82.9

5. Write down 2 numbers between:

(a) 3.3 and 3.6
(b) 3.5 and 3.7
(c) 7.8 and 8
(d) 9 and 9.2
(e) 45.1 and 45.4
(f) 48.8 and 49
(g) 39.8 and 40
(h) 99.8 and 100

6. Write down 10 numbers between:

(a) 3.2 and 3.5
(b) 5.2 and 5.5
(c) 9.1 and 9.4
(d) 0.7 and 1
(e) 32.6 and 32.8
(f) 40 and 40.3
(g) 38 and 40
(h) 89.5 and 90

7. Write down the most important things to think about when writing numbers between other numbers.

Decimals on number lines

Copy each of these number lines into your books. On as many lines as possible mark in the following decimals. 1.5, 0.2, 0.25, 0.7, 3.2

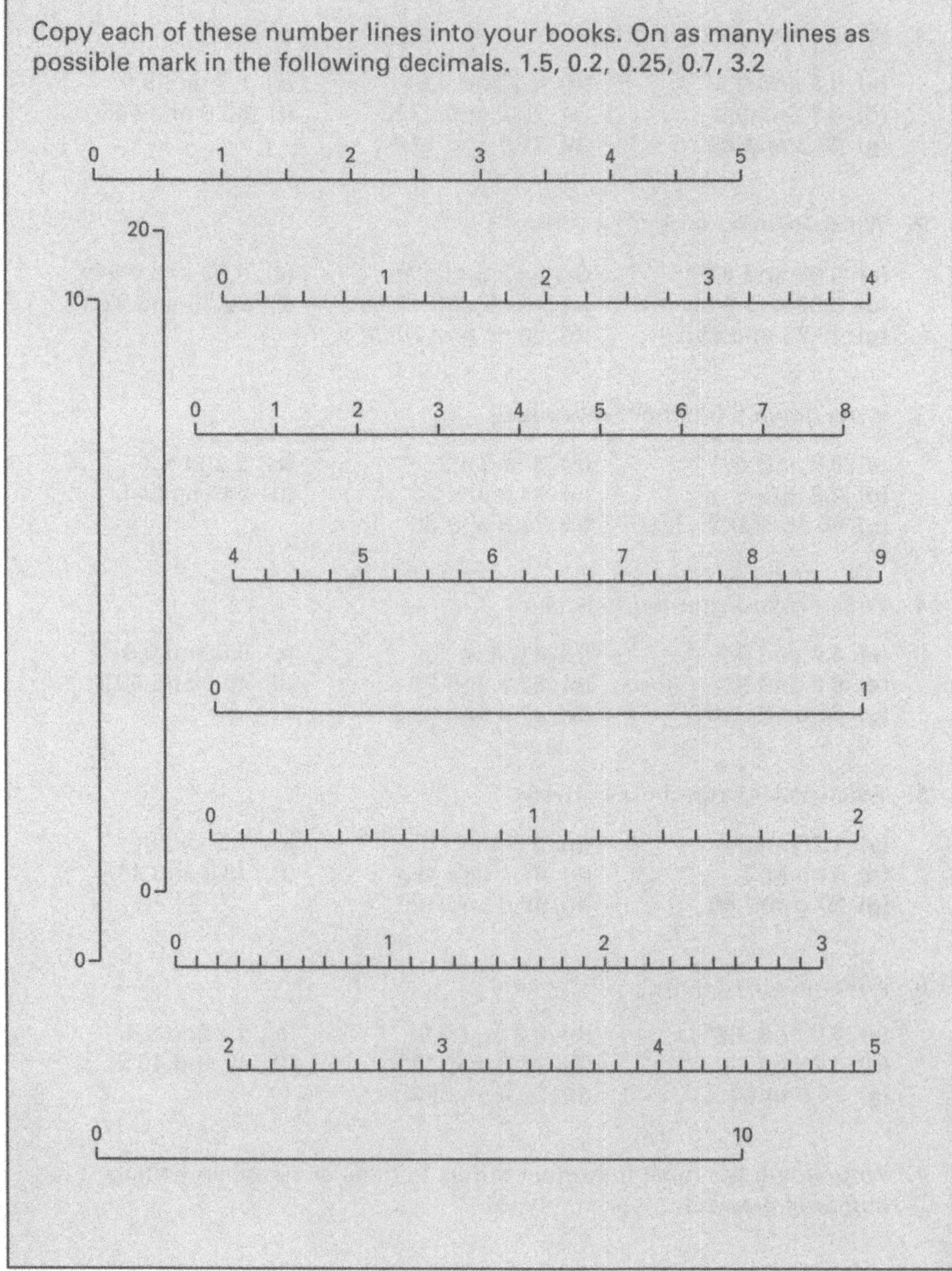

Ordering decimals

1. Which is larger?

   (a) 0.7 or 0.9 (b) 0.3 or 0.1 (c) 0.5 or 0.3
   (d) 0.8 or 0.9 (e) 21.3 or 32.1 (f) 81.2 or 39.7
   (g) 21.3 or 19.8 (h) 15.7 or 14.9

2. Which is larger?

   (a) 4.12 or 3.61 (b) 3.25 or 5.12 (c) 9.12 or 9.03
   (d) 8.83 or 9.51 (e) 35.63 or 38.41 (f) 43.12 or 39.98
   (g) 61.23 or 58.73 (h) 86.32 or 91.12

3. Write down the largest of the three numbers.

   (a) 0.7, 0.2, 0.6 (b) 0.3, 0.8, 0.1 (c) 0.1, 0.5, 0.2
   (d) 1.3, 5.1, 2.0 (e) 23.75, 23.12, 22.18 (f) 0.32, 0.87, 0.51
   (g) 15.15, 80.02, 39.98 (h) 41.13, 52, 47.36

4. Which is larger?

   (a) 4.5 or 7 (b) 9. or 2.1 (c) 5 or 4.5
   (d) 8.6 or 10 (e) 28.7 or 32 (f) 35 or 28.8
   (g) 50 or 49.8 (h) 68.5 or 71

5. Which is larger?

   (a) 1.25 or 2 (b) 3 or 2.75 (c) 8 or 8.25
   (d) 2.25 or 2 (e) 32.55 or 40 (f) 75 or 72.88
   (g) 80 or 78.95 (h) 20.25 or 71

6. Which is larger?

   (a) 0.5 or 0.25 (b) 5.5 or 5.25 (c) 7.1 or 6.75
   (d) 4.25 or 6.1 (e) 28.5 or 28.75 (f) 35.1 or 35.25
   (g) 80.5 or 80.25 (h) 76.2 or 73.75

7. Write down the most important thing to think about when choosing the bigger of two decimals.

Patterns with decimals

Copy the following into your book and write in numbers that continue the pattern.

1. 0.1 0.2 0.3 0.4 ____ ____ ____.
2. 0.5 1.0 1.5 2.0 2.5 ____ ____ ____.
3. 10 9.5 9.0 8.5 8.0 ____ ____ ____.
4. 0 1.5 3.0 4.5 ____ ____ ____.
5. 101 100.8 100.6 100.4 ____ ____ ____ ____ ____.
6. 0.25 0.5 0.75 1 1.25 ____ ____ ____.
7. 0.05 0.15 0.25 0.35 ____ ____ ____.
8. 10 8.5 7 5.5 ____ ____ ____.
9. 50 50.5 51 51.5 ____ ____ ____.
10. 0.6 1.2 1.8 2.4 3.0 ____ ____ ____.
11. 1.1 1.15 1.2 1.25 1.3 ____ ____ ____.
12. 12 12.05 12.1 12.15 12.2 ____ ____ ____.
13. 10.6 10.7 10.8 10.9 ____ ____ ____.
14. 10.5 20.5 30.5 40.5 ____ ____ ____.
15. 1 200 1 200.1 1 200.2 1 200.3 ____ ____ ____.

Hidden patterns

In the following patterns, some of the elements have been covered up. In each case, calculate how many elements are covered.

1.

2.

3.

4.

Different words for multiplication

1. What is 23 multiplied by 6?

2. What is 35 times 10?

3. In my plantation I have 25 rows of trees, and there are 9 trees in each row. How many trees is that altogether?

4. In my school there are 242 students. Each pupil has 3 books, how many books is that altogether?

5. In my garden I have planted 35 tomato plants. My friend has 7 times as many tomato plants as me. How many tomato plants does my friend have?

6. In a hall, there are 35 seats in each row and 60 rows. How many seats are there altogether?

7. One plane ticket costs K215. How much would 12 of those tickets cost?

8. Each of my paces is 75 cm long. How far will I walk if I take 30 paces?

9. This list shows the price of some gardening tools.

Pick	K43
Wheelbarrow	K136
Shovel	K15
Hoe	K28

(a) How much does it cost to buy 12 picks?

(b) How much would 6 wheelbarrows cost?

(c) What would be the total cost of 1 wheelbarrow, 3 picks, 5 shovels and 8 hoes?

Multiplication story problems

1. On December 15th I sent a package by freight. The package, which was tied together with 4 pieces of string, weighed 15 kg. For each kilogram I had to pay K12. How much did I pay altogether?
2. Each PNG kina can buy 36 Japanese yen and 2 300 Indonesian rupiah. It is possible to change money in banks. How many Japanese yen can I buy at the bank with K6?
3. A Boeing 737 can travel at 650 km per hour. How far can the Boeing 737 travel in 12 hours?
4. I have 15 pigs altogether. One of the sows has 7 piglets. After they have grown a little, I can sell the piglets for K23 each. How much can I make if I sell all of these piglets?

5. In the first film night of the year there were 65 adults who paid K3 and 120 children who paid K2 each. On the second film night there were 82 adults, and 176 children. How much did the adults pay altogether on the first night?
6. When travelling on Air Nuigini a passenger is allowed 16 kg of baggage free of charge. For every kilogram of baggage over 16 kg an excess baggage fee is charged. Delin's baggage weighed 20 kg. How much excess baggage did she have? For her journey Air Nuigini charged an excess baggage fee of K5 per kilogram. How much did Delin have to pay?
7. Esta wanted to buy some onions to sell at the market. A string bag of onions costs K28.00. Esta decided to buy three bags. How much did Esta have to pay altogether?
8. Alena weaves mats from pandanus leaves. She sells them for K 20 each. Last month Alena sold ten mats. How much did she earn?
9. Make up a question like question 5 and ask a friend to work out the answer. Did they get it correct?

Matching up multiplication

Copy these tables into your books, and fill in the empty spaces.

1.

Problem	In words	Using symbols	Answer
	12 multiplied by 20		
Each box of matches holds 50 matches. How many matches would 35 boxes hold?			
		5 x 200	
			600
How many seconds are there in 35 minutes?			
		155 x 20	

2.

Problem	Diagram	Using words	Symbols
Each tin of tomatoes holds 16 tomatoes. How many tomatoes would 25 tins hold?			
	□□□□□□□□□□□□□□ □□□□□□□□□□□□□□ □□□□□□□□□□□□□□ □□□□□□□□□□□□□□		
		6 rows of 15	
			8 x15
In a plane there are 32 rows of seats and 7 seats in each row. How many people can sit in the plane?			
	******************* ******************* ******************* ******************* ******************* *******************		

Multiplication short cuts

Copy the questions into your books and write the answer as a number sentence (**do the calculation in your head**).

e.g. 35 x 10 = 350

1. **(a)** 23 x 10 **(b)** 87 x 10 **(c)** 45 x 10
(d) 60 x 10 **(e)** 230 x 10 **(f)** 850 x 10
(g) 300 x 10 **(h)** 123 x 10

2. **(a)** 6 x 20 **(b)** 6 x 50 **(c)** 8 x 40
(d) 3 x 90 **(e)** 10 x 20 **(f)** 15 x 20
(g) 25 x 40 **(h)** 50 x 20

3. **(a)** 7 x 100 **(b)** 15 x 100 **(c)** 23 x 100
(d) 72 x 100 **(e)** 57 x 100 **(f)** 70 x 100
(g) 81 x 100 **(h)** 45 x 100

4. **(a)** 4 x 1 000 **(b)** 7 x 1 000 **(c)** 12 x 1 000
(d) 15 x 1 000 **(e)** 23 x 1 000 **(f)** 49 x 1 000
(g) 30 x 1 000 **(h)** 125 x 1 000

5. **(a)** 4 x 200 **(b)** 9 x 200 **(c)** 5 x 400
(d) 6 x 500 **(e)** 4 x 2 000 **(f)** 7 x 2 000
(g) 5 x 3 000 **(h)** 12 x 5 000

6. **(a)** 20 x 30 **(b)** 20 x 40 **(c)** 50 x 30
(d) 80 x 30 **(e)** 20 x 90 **(f)** 40 x 50
(g) 60 x 50 **(h)** 80 x 50

7. **(a)** 7 x 99 **(b)** 4 x 99 **(c)** 11 x 99
(d) 15 x 99 **(e)** 7 x 999 **(f)** 5 x 999
(g) 3 x 999 **(h)** 8 x 999

8. Write down the most important thing to think about when multiplying numbers in your head.

How many times?

How many times will the container on the left fill each container on the right?

	(a)	(b)	(c)
1. 200 mL	600 mL	1 Litre	800 mL
2. 250 mL	750 mL	500 mL	1 Litre
3. 500 mL	2 Litres	1.5 L	5 Litres
4. 50 mL	100 mL	500 mL	250 mL
5. 100 mL	1 Litre	600 mL	500 mL

Working out quantities

1. I am making a fruit drink using the following:

(a) $\frac{1}{4}$ litre of orange juice

(b) $\frac{1}{2}$ litre of apple juice

(c) $1\frac{1}{4}$ litres of dry ginger

(d) $\frac{3}{4}$ litre of lemonade

(e) $\frac{1}{10}$ litre of water

(f) $\frac{1}{5}$ litre of soda water

(g) $2\frac{1}{5}$ litres of mineral water

(h) $\frac{3}{10}$ litre of grape juice

For each one, write the amount in millilitres. How much drink have I made altogether?

2. Write each amount as millilitres.

(a) 0.5 L	(b) 1.25 L	(c) 0.375 L	(d) 2.75 L
(e) 1.455 L	(f) 2.875 L	(g) 0.8 L	(h) 0.738 L
(i) 3.5 L	(j) 2.25 L	(k) 1.235 L	(l) 2.675 L
(m) 0.567 L	(n) 1.642 L	(o) 3.2 L	(p) 1.8 L

3. Use decimal notation to write these quantities as litres.

(a) 250 mL	(b) 1 500 mL	(c) 325 mL	(d) 750 mL
(e) 4 675 mL	(f) 1 725 mL	(g) 600 mL	(h) 675 mL
(i) 456 mL	(j) 2 125 mL	(k) 835 mL	(l) 1 250 mL
(m) 385 ml	(n) 915 mL	(o) 2 565 mL	(p) 1 200 mL

Fill the container

Which containers on the right would together fill the one on the left?

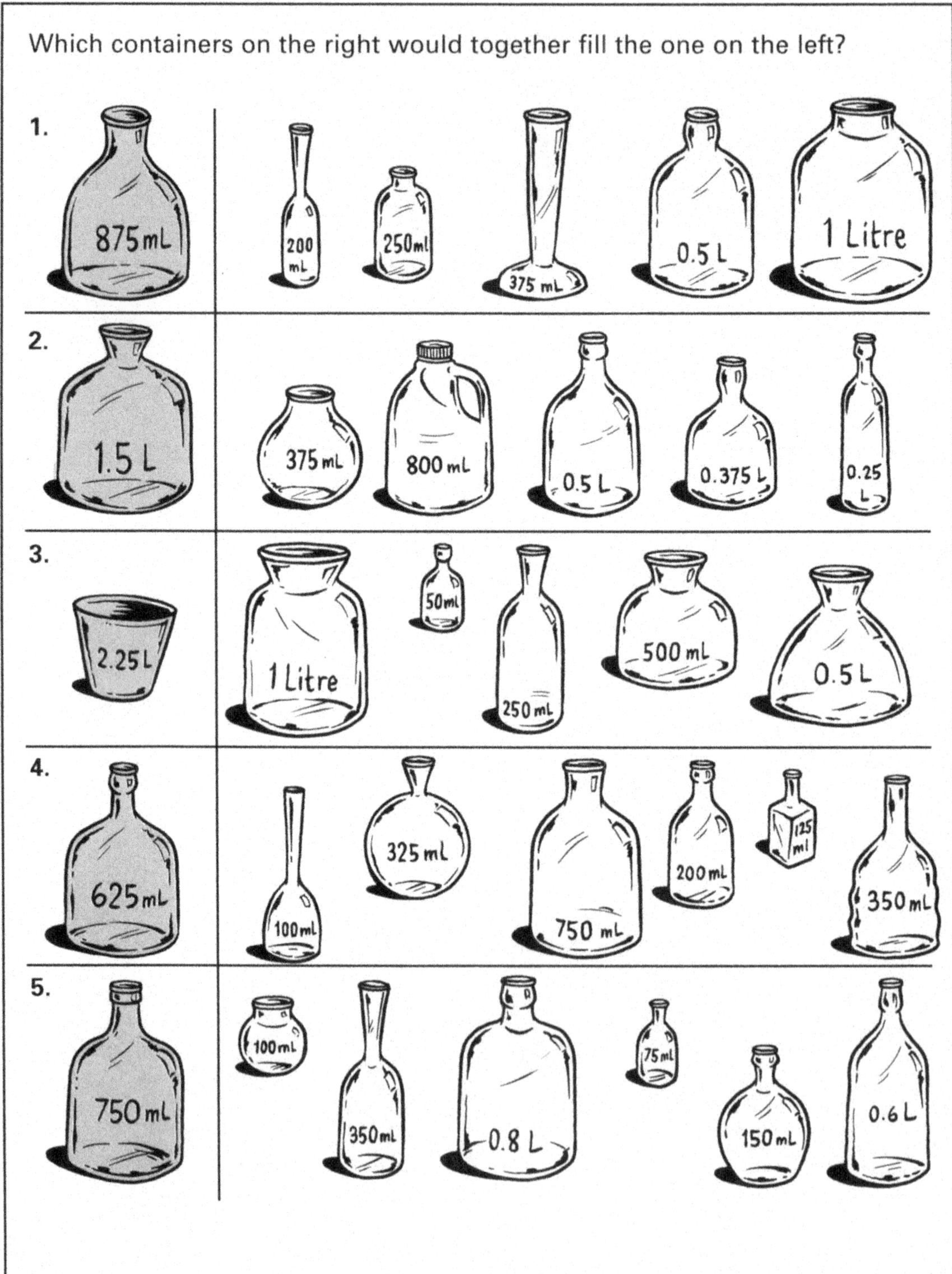

Which is the better buy?

Both sets of products are the same price. Work out the volume of each set to find which is the better buy.

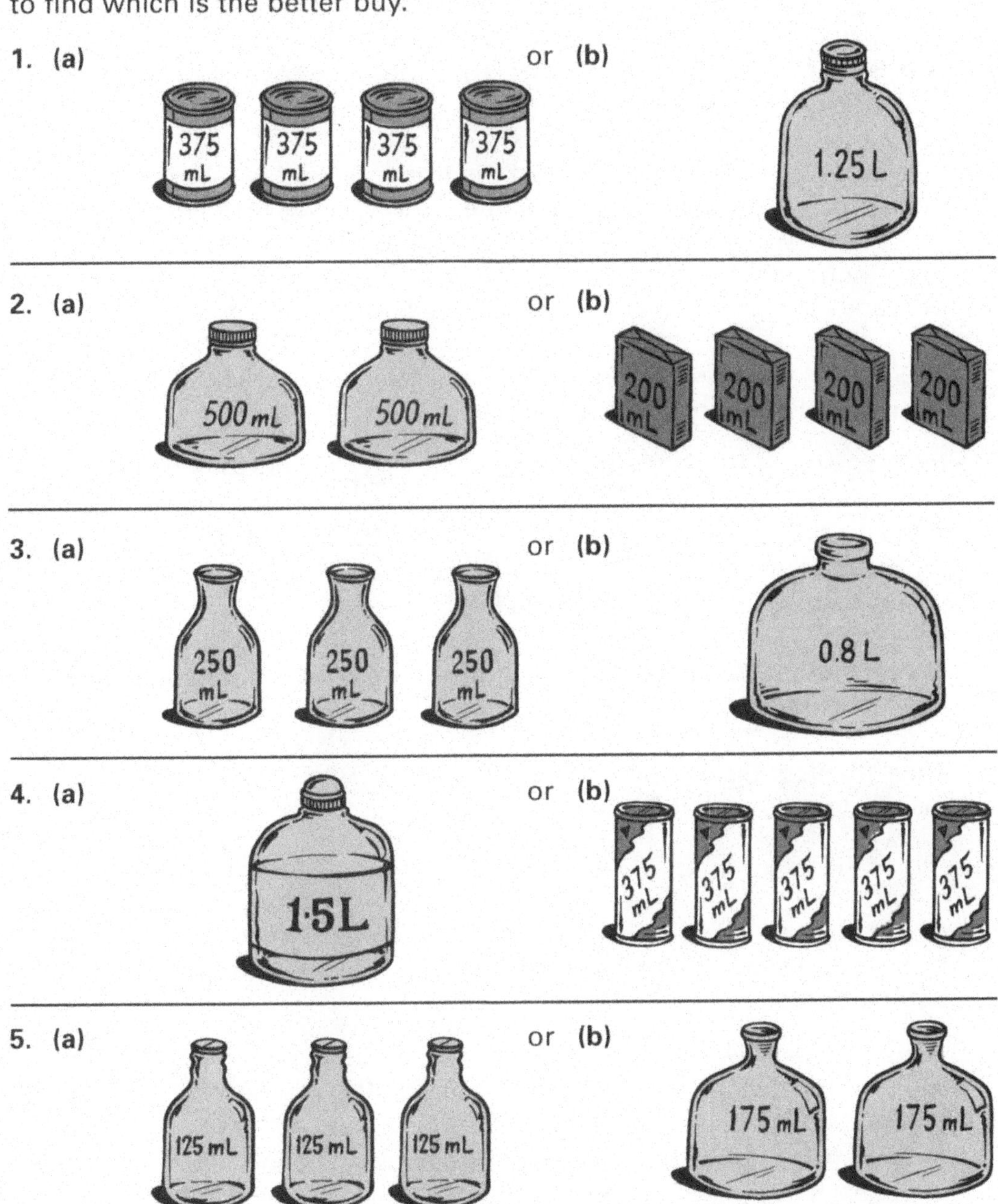

Solving word problems 1

Capacity and volume

1. When Julius went to the doctor he was given some medicine. He was to take 5 mL of medicine three times a day for eight days. How much medicine did he take altogether?

2. Sam was given a 100 mL bottle of medicine. He had to take 5 mL four times a day. How many days until the medicine was finished?

3. Each morning the five people in the Ovasuru family drink 200 mL each of orange juice. How many days would a 5 litre container of juice last?

4. If 25 school children each drink 400 mL of water each day, how many litres would they drink altogether in:

   (a) 1 week? **(b)** 15 days? **(c)** 25 days?

5. A bucket holds 10 litres of water. If I pour 875 mL into one container, 650 mL into another container, 2.75 L into another container, and 1.5 L into a fourth container, how much is still left in the bucket?

6. My car needed 22 litres of petrol to fill it. If petrol costs K1.80 per litre, how much did I pay?

7. I use 10 mL of disinfectant in every 2 litres of water. How much disinfectant do I need for:

   (a) 10 litres? **(b)** 12 litres? **(c)** 40 litres?

8. Liquid plant food has to be diluted with water so that for every 2 litres of water you use 5 mL of liquid plant food. How much liquid plant food do I need for:

   (a) 10 litres of water? **(b)** 5 litres of water?
   (c) 14 litres of water? **(d)** 50 litres of water?

9. A rainwater tank holds 5 000 litres. If each person uses about 5 litres of water each day, how long would the tank last a village with 30 people if there was no rain?

Solving word problems 2

Capacity and volume

1. Darusila wanted to fill 28 drink bottles each holding 750 mL. How many large bottles of drink each holding 2 litres does she need to buy in order to fill all the small drink bottles?

2. If I buy a 2 litre container of milk, how long will it last if I drink 250 mL each day?

3. On a trip, my car used 15 litres of petrol. My car travels 8 kilometres for every litre of petrol. How many kilometres was the trip?

4. If a truck uses 1 litre of diesel every 10 kilometres, how many litres will it use if I travel:

   (a) 300 kilometres? **(b)** 85 kilometres? **(c)** 220 kilometres?

5. If it takes 10 seconds to fill a 2 litre container, how long will it take to fill fifty 2 litre containers?

6. A dripping tap produces 25 mL of water every 30 seconds. How much water would be wasted in:

   (a) 1 hour? **(b)** 1 day? **(c)** 1 week?

7. If water comes out of a tap at a rate of 2 litres in half a minute, how long will it take to fill a:

   (a) 10 litre container? **(b)** 24 litre container?

8. A water tank holds 20 000 litres of water. How many 10 litre buckets can be filled from the tank?

Moving people in groups

Write the answers to these questions as sentences.

1. A class of 40 students want to travel by canoe. Each canoe can hold 12 students. How many canoes are needed?
2. 34 people need to cross a river. There are 6 canoes available and each canoe can hold up to 8 people. How would you arrange the people?
3. 74 people want to travel to town for a special church service. The village PMV can only hold 20 people. How many trips must the PMV make?

4. 74 students want to travel to Goroka by bus. The school has hired 5 buses, and each bus holds a maximum of 20 students. How would you arrange the students on the buses?
5. 46 people want to travel from Balimo to Kiunga by plane. The plane can hold 8 people. How many trips are necessary?
6. There are 34 students in a grade. The teacher wants to take them on a picnic to an island. The school dinghy holds 6. How many trips are necessary?
7. 24 women want to perform a traditional dance. They have to stand in rows. How many rows can they form?

Matching up division

Copy these tables into your book, and fill in the empty spaces. Each line must be a different way of presenting the same calculation.

1.

Problem	In words	Calculation	Symbols
	eight hundred and twenty divided by twenty		
I want to walk to a place 52 km away. I can walk 4 km each hour. How many hours will it take me to walk to that place?			
			200 ÷ 7
		$30\overline{)240}$	
How long is 100 hours, expressed in days?			
		$20\overline{)155}$	

2.

Problem	In words	Calculation	Symbols
In our school there are 188 students. How many basketball teams of 5 students can we make?			
			360 ÷ 24
		$6\overline{)460}$	
	seventeen divided by four		
How many weeks are there in 1 000 days?			
		$4\overline{)19}$	

Different words for division

1. What is 48 divided by 6?
2. How many 6s are there in 94?

3. In my plantation I want to have 287 trees, and 7 rows. How many trees do I need to plant in each row?
4. In my school there are 242 students. How many groups of 3 students are there?
5. In my school there are 216 students. If there are 4 houses for sports, how many students will there be in each house?
6. In my garden I have planted 364 peanut plants. I have 7 times as many peanut plants as my friend. How many peanut plants does my friend have?

7. In a hall, there are 360 chairs altogether. There is room for 30 rows. How many chairs should I put in each row?
8. 8 friends have decided to combine to buy a present and share the cost equally. Their present costs K216. How much does each person need to contribute?
9. A group of 5 friends go fishing. They agree to share the fish equally. Altogether they caught 113 fish. How many fish does each person get?
10. 20 tents were put up for a Christian women's leadership rally. A hundred women attended the rally and the organisers of the rally wanted the same number of women to sleep in each tent. How many women slept in each tent?
11. In a volleyball championship all the towns and villages that took part fielded a team of 6 players and 3 reserves. Altogether there were 108 players and reserves. How many towns and villages sent a team to take part in the championship?

Division story problems with extra numbers

1. I want to save K530 to travel to visit my relatives in 12 months time. I get paid K100 each fortnight. How much do I need to save each month?

2. A box of 6 radios weighs 3 kilograms and costs K268. How much does each radio cost?
3. A rectangular garden is 5 metres wide, has 120 plants, and has an area of 84 square metres. How long is the garden?
4. A Fokker F28 airplane needs to travel 490 kilometres in 3 hours. How far must it fly each hour?
5. In an election there are 860 voters, 4 candidates, 12 voting places, and 2 days for voting. If the votes were evenly shared, how many votes would each candidate get?

6. Make up a question like question 5 and ask a friend to work out the answer. Was your friend correct?
7. A Toyota Hilux needs to travel a distance of 260 kilometres in 5 hours. What distance must it travel each hour?

Division short cuts

Copy the questions into your books and write the answer as a number sentence (**do the calculation in your head**).

e.g. 350 ÷ 10 = 35

1. **(a)** 230 ÷ 10 **(b)** 870 ÷ 10 **(c)** 450 ÷ 10
(d) 600 ÷ 10 **(e)** 2 330 ÷ 10 **(f)** 8 700 ÷ 10
(g) 4 550 ÷ 10 **(h)** 6 000 ÷ 10

2. **(a)** 600 ÷ 2 **(b)** 270 ÷ 3 **(c)** 240 ÷ 4
(d) 450 ÷ 9 **(e)** 560 ÷ 7 **(f)** 350 ÷ 5
(g) 360 ÷ 4 **(h)** 420 ÷ 6

3. **(a)** 6 000 ÷ 2 **(b)** 3 600 ÷ 3 **(c)** 2 800 ÷ 4
(d) 8 100 ÷ 9 **(e)** 6 800 ÷ 2 **(f)** 3 300 ÷ 3
(g) 3 200 ÷ 4 **(h)** 2 700 ÷ 9

4. **(a)** 600 ÷ 20 **(b)** 250 ÷ 50 **(c)** 320 ÷ 40
(d) 180 ÷ 90 **(e)** 260 ÷ 20 **(f)** 350 ÷ 50
(g) 240 ÷ 40 **(h)** 320 ÷ 20

5. **(a)** 3 000 ÷ 20 **(b)** 3 100 ÷ 20 **(c)** 3 080 ÷ 20
(d) 3 500 ÷ 20 **(e)** 6 600 ÷ 20 **(f)** 6 700 ÷ 20
(g) 6 080 ÷ 20 **(h)** 6 500 ÷ 20

6 **(a)** 4 500 ÷ 50 **(b)** 6 000 ÷ 50 **(c)** 2 000 ÷ 50
(d) 3 000 ÷ 50 **(e)** 2 500 ÷ 50 **(f)** 1 000 ÷ 50
(g) 2 000 ÷ 40 **(h)** 3 200 ÷ 40

7. Write down the most important thing to think about when dividing numbers in your head.

Kilograms or grams?

1. Copy each product name into your book and write whether it is grams or kilograms.

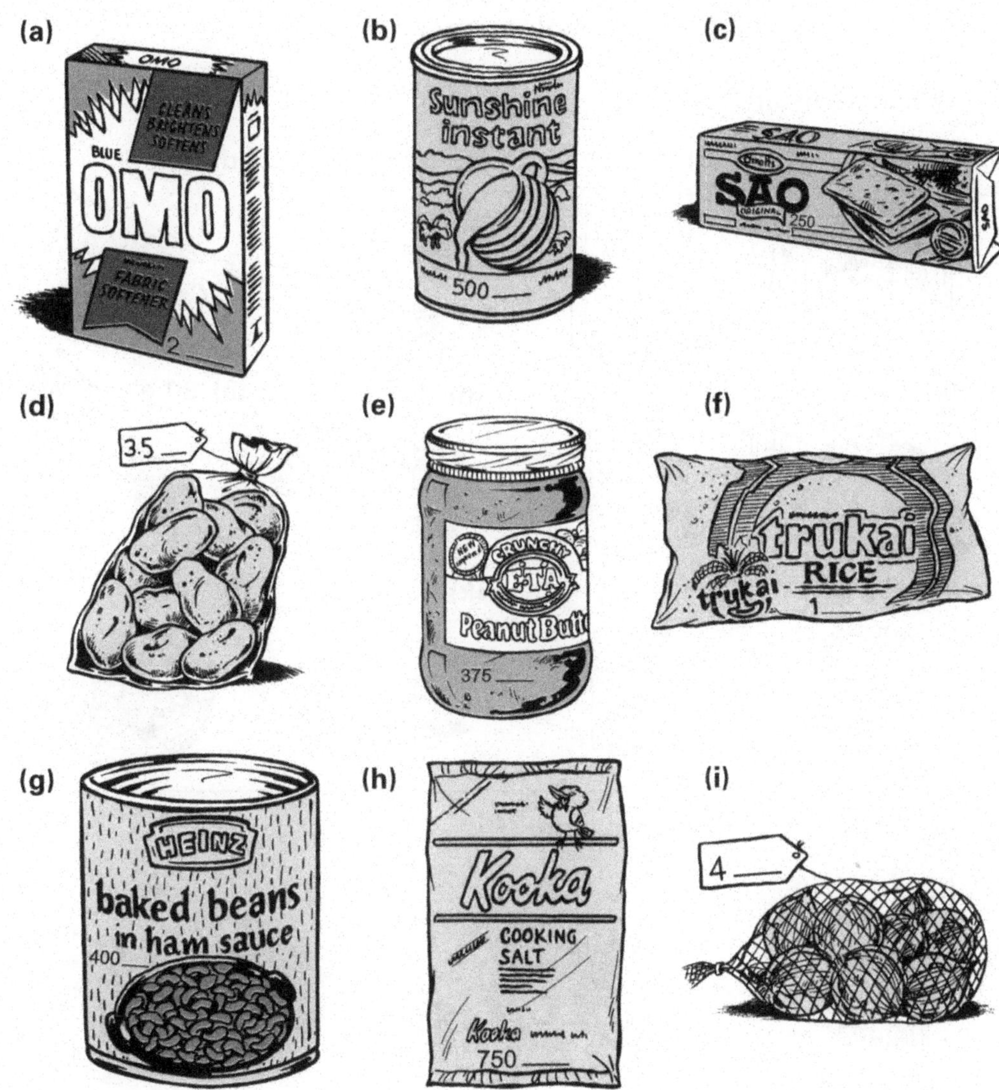

2. What unit of weight would you use to measure:

   (a) a person? **(b)** a letter? **(c)** a cup of sugar?
   (d) a suitcase of luggage? **(e)** a bucket? **(f)** a pig?
   (g) a drinking glass? **(h)** a dog?

Fractions of a kilogram

1. Which items are more than $\frac{1}{2}$ kilogram?

   Which items are less than $\frac{1}{5}$ kilogram?

   Which items are less than $\frac{1}{10}$ kilogram?

   (a) 50 g (b) 750 g (c) 375 g (d) 100 g

   (e) 560 g (f) 85 g (g) 700 g (h) 30 g

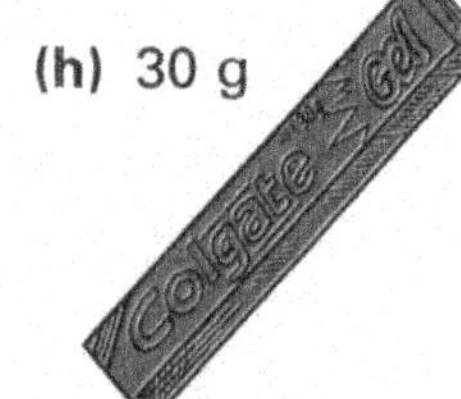

   (i) 155 g (j) 910 g (k) 170 g (l) 250 g

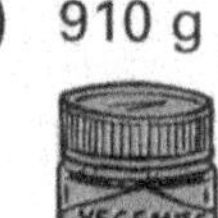

2. For each pair, which weighs more?

   (a) $\frac{3}{4}$ kg $\frac{1}{4}$ kg (b) $\frac{1}{5}$ kg $\frac{1}{2}$ kg

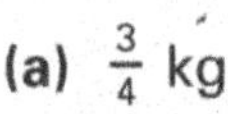

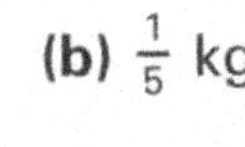
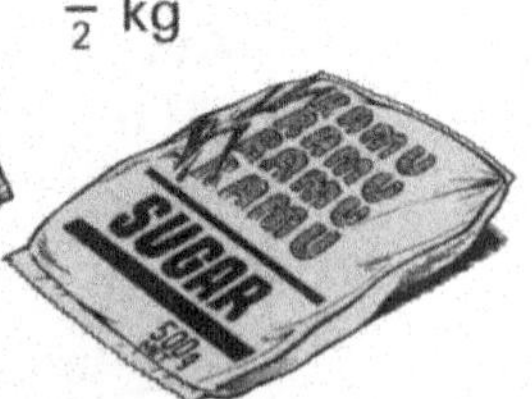

   (c) $\frac{1}{2}$ kg $\frac{2}{5}$ kg (d) $\frac{3}{4}$ kg $\frac{4}{5}$ kg

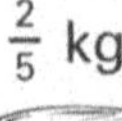

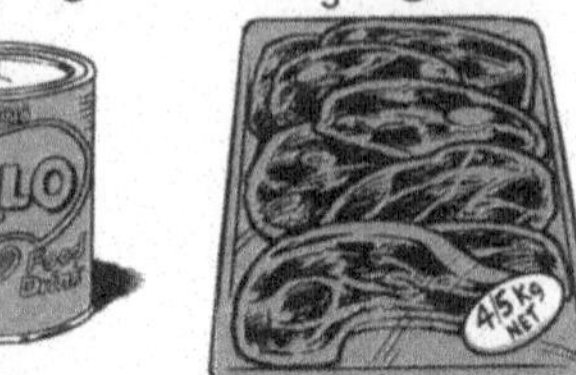

More fractions of a kilogram

1. How many grams?

(a) $\frac{1}{4}$ kg butter

(b) $\frac{1}{5}$ kg beans

(c) $\frac{1}{2}$ kg flour

(d) $\frac{3}{4}$ kg sugar

(e) $\frac{2}{5}$ kg peanuts

(f) $\frac{1}{10}$ kg salt

(g) $\frac{9}{10}$ kg rice

In each case how much more do you need to make 1 kg?

2. How many grams?

(a) $1\frac{3}{4}$ kg potatoes

(b) $2\frac{1}{2}$ kg onions

(c) $1\frac{1}{5}$ kg butter

(d) $2\frac{1}{4}$ kg fruit

(e) $1\frac{3}{10}$ kg bananas

(f) $1\frac{1}{2}$ kg flour

(g) $1\frac{1}{4}$ kg coffee

In each case how much more do you need to make 5 kg?

3. Write each of these amounts as a fraction of a kilogram:

(a) 500 g (b) 250 g (c) 100 g
(d) 200 g (e) 750 g

4. Change these grams to kilograms and fractions of kilograms:

(a) 1 500 g (b) 3 500 g (c) 1 200 g (d) 2 750 g
(e) 3 100 g (f) 1 250 g (g) 1 750 g (h) 1 100 g

5. Write each of these amounts as kilograms and grams.

(a) 1.200 kg (b) 3.400 kg (c) 5.550 kg (d) 0.575 kg
(e) 3.200 kg (f) 3.250 kg (g) 0.050 kg (h) 1.125 kg

Trucking along

Use the gross and tare weights to find the maximum weight each vehicle is permitted to carry.

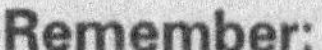

Remember:

Gross weight = total weight of the vehicle and its contents.
Tare weight = the weight of the empty vehicle.
Net weight = the weight of the contents.

(a)
Gross = 1 500 kg
Tare = 1 t

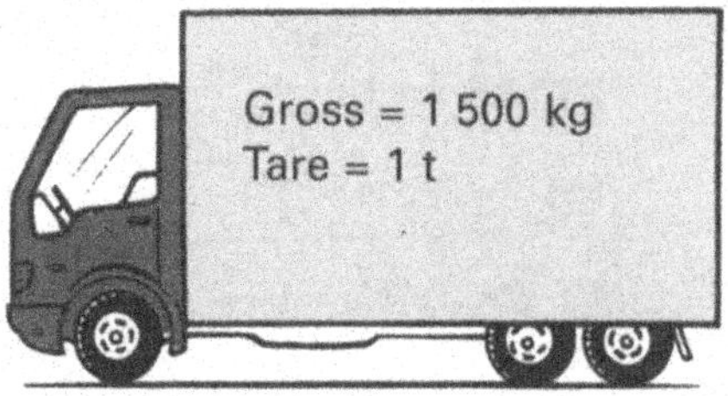

(b)
Gross = 4 700 kg
Tare = 2 435 kg

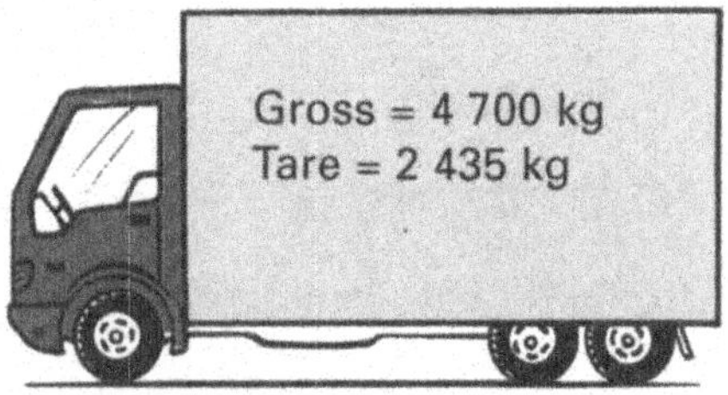

(c)
Gross = 5 t
Tare = 1 300 kg

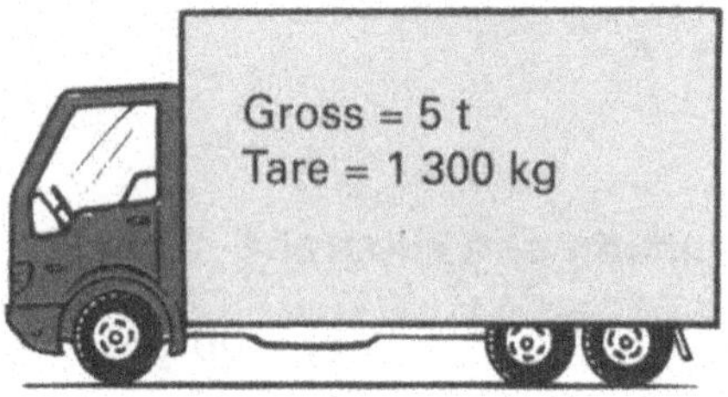

(d)
Gross = 3.5 t
Tare = 1 350 kg

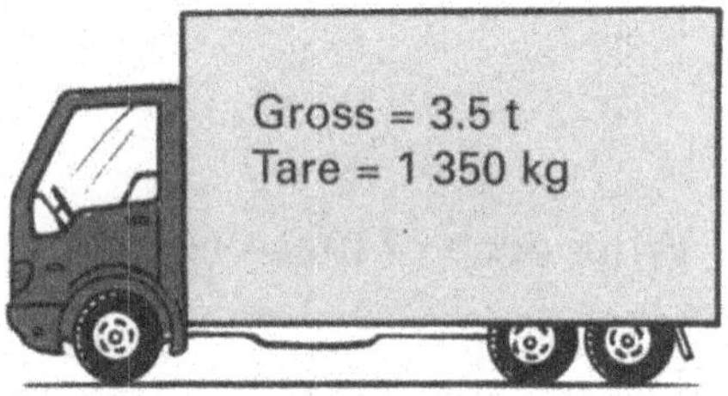

(e)
Gross = 1 200 kg
Tare = 3 000 kg

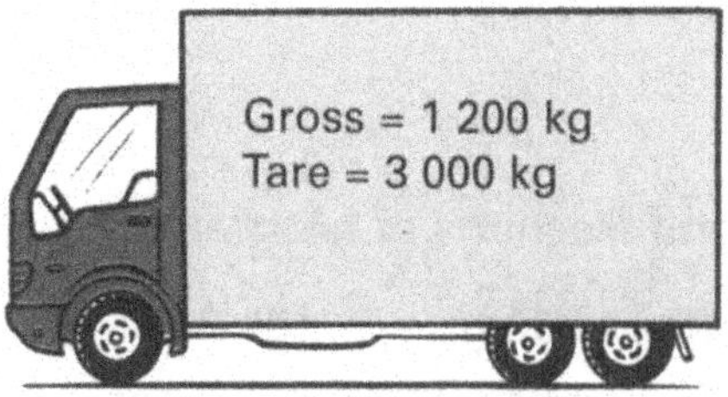

(f)
Gross = 2.75 t
Tare = 900 kg

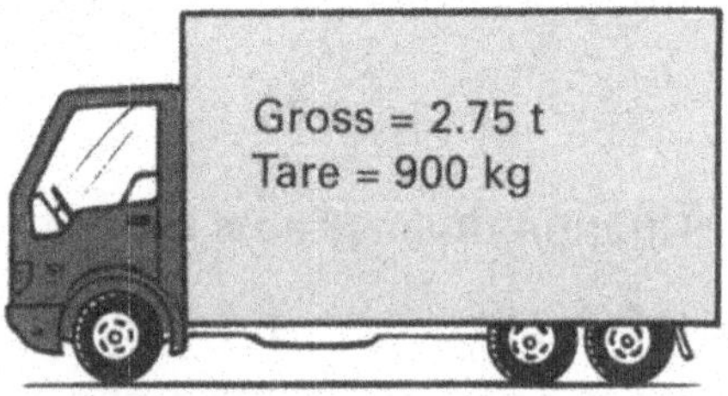

(g)
Gross = 5.25 t
Tare = 2 500 kg

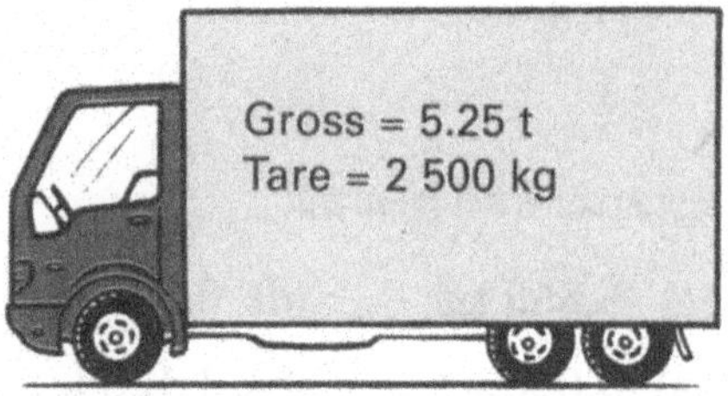

(h)
Gross = 3.8 t
Tare = 1.2 t

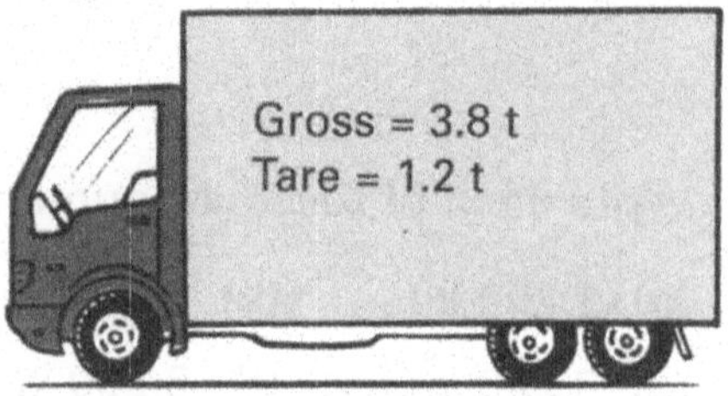

Using decimals

1. Write as grams:

(a) 1.675 kg	(b) 0.588 kg	(c) 1.2 kg	(d) 0.6 kg
(e) 3.75 kg	(f) 1.395 kg	(g) 4.075 kg	(h) 2.5 kg
(i) 5.9 kg	(j) 2.156 kg	(k) 1.962 kg	(l) 0.3 kg

2. Write as a decimal fraction of a kilogram:

(a) 2 500 g	(b) 1 250 g	(c) 3 627 g	(d) 1 785 g
(e) 2 950 g	(f) 1 675 g	(g) 295 g	(h) 817 g
(i) 1 075 g	(j) 3 400 g	(k) 2 100 g	(l) 1 750 g

3. Write as kilograms:

(a) 2.125 t	(b) 1.5 t	(c) 3.615 t	(d) 4.7 t
(e) 5.5 t	(f) 0.856 t	(g) 3.2 t	(h) 0.75 t
(i) 1.25 t	(j) 2.6 t	(k) 1.9 t	(l) 0.395 t

4. Write as a decimal fraction of a tonne:

(a) 156 kg	(b) 2 500 kg	(c) 1 125 kg	(d) 975 kg
(e) 3 450 kg	(f) 1 750 kg	(g) 500 kg	(h) 1 095 kg
(i) 3 200 kg	(j) 2 250 kg	(k) 1 355 kg	(l) 250 kg

5. How many grams are there in:

(a) 1 t	(b) 3 t	(c) 5 t	(d) 0.5 t
(e) 0.8 t	(f) 0.2 t	(g) 0.25 t	(h) 0.6 t
(i) 1.5 t	(j) 2.5 t	(k) 0.1 t	(l) 1.2 t?

6. One cement bag weighs 25 kg. How much will 100 bags weigh? (Write your answer in two different ways.)

7. A truck that can carry 2 tonnes, has a load of 50 boxes. How much does each box weigh?

Adding and subtracting weight

Decide if you need to add or subtract before you solve each problem.

1. A loaded truck has a weight of 17 t. When unloaded its weight is 3.9 t. What was the weight of the load?

2. When my suitcase was weighed it was 21.375 kg. I was allowed 26 kg. How much more weight could I have packed?
3. Rena weighed her dog by holding it while she stood on the scales. Together they weighed 75.5 kilograms. Rena knew she weighed 52.25 kg. How much did her dog weigh?
4. Mrs. Melawi bought 0.7 kg flour, 1.35 kg rice, 2.675 kg sweet potatoes, and 0.115 kg ginger. The shopkeeper put them in a plastic carry bag. How heavy was the load?
5. Three containers were to be loaded on to a ship. One was 6.725 t, another was 2.036 t, and the third was 3.5 t. What was their total weight?

6. A mining truck can carry 75 tonnes of copper ore. The first load put in the truck was 29.435 t and the second load was 36.9 t. How much more ore could the truck have carried?
7. A village produced 16.75 kg tomatoes, 11.4 kg beans, 0.5 t kaukau and 0.1 t peanuts. What is the total weight of the village's produce?

Recording money amounts

How much money?

1. (a)

(b)

(c)

2. Write these amounts as kina.

(a) 547t (b) 213t (c) 459t (d) 360t
(e) 753t (f) 108t (g) 639t (h) 256t

3. Work out how much money and then write it as kina.

(a) 25 ten toea coins
(b) 30 fifty toea coins
(c) 15 twenty toea coins
(d) 100 two toea coins
(e) 50 five toea coins
(f) 10 twenty toea coins
(g) 26 twenty toea coins
(h) 36 ten toea coins

Things to buy

Which products can you buy with:

(a) K20? **(b)** K25? **(c)** K50? **(d)** K75? **(e)** K100?

How much change will you get from each amount?

Which is cheapest?

1. Here are lists of supplies from four stores. Which store has the cheapest overall price?

Walaka's Store	
Roofing iron (per sheet)	K23.50
Nails (per packet)	K3.60
Roofing nails (per kg)	K8.00
Weather board (per metre)	K3.00
Tape measure	K28.00
Hammer	K20.00
Total	

Joe's Store	
Roofing iron (per sheet)	K20.50
Nails (per packet)	K4.80
Roofing nails (per kg)	K7.50
Weather board (per metre)	K3.50
Tape measure	K22.75
Hammer	K15.95
Total	

Tau's Store	
Roofing iron (per sheet)	K19.85
Nails (per packet)	K5.00
Roofing nails (per kg)	K8.50
Weather board (per metre)	K2.75
Tape measure	K37.50
Hammer	K27.50
Total	

Rodi's Store	
Roofing iron (per sheet)	K21.00
Nails (per packet)	K3.20
Roofing nails (per kg)	K7.20
Weather board (per metre)	K2.00
Tape measure	K56.00
Hammer	K29.75
Total	

2. Make a list of your own using the cheapest price for each item from the four stores. Use your own list to work out how much it will cost to buy:

   (a) 50 m of weather board, 2 sheets of roofing iron, 1 kg of roofing nails and 2 packets of nails.

   (b) 4 sheets of roofing iron, 150 m of weather board and 1 hammer.

   (c) 1 tape measure, 1 hammer, 3 kg of roofing nails and 5 packets of nails.

   (d) 100 m of weather board, 4 packets of nails, 1 hammer, 1 tape measure.

Value for money?

In each case work out which size product is better value and record it in your own book.

How much do you save?

	Regular price	Sale price
	Regular price K3.99	Sale price K2.49
	Regular price K14.99	Sale price K13.99
	Regular price K2.30	Sale price K2.19
	Regular price K2.54	Sale price K2.35
	Regular price K2.98	Sale price K2.54
	Regular price K1.54	Sale price K1.48
	Regular price K5.12	Sale price K4.98
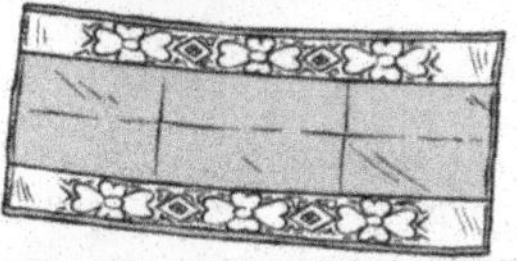	Regular price K12.80	Sale price K10.99

1. For each item work out the difference between the regular price and the sale price to find out how much you save.
2. If you bought all these products before the sale how much would you pay?
3. If you bought them all during the sale how much would you pay?
4. What is your total saving?

Word problems

1. How much change would I get from K10 if I bought 2 packets of tea at 99t each, and 1 kg plain flour at K1.29?
2. If I bought 4 tins of milk powder at K5.35 per tin, how much would I pay?
3. If 1 kg of Ramu sugar costs K2.30, how much is 100 g worth?
4. How much will 2 packets of biscuits at K3.99 each, 2 tins of corned beef at K2.89 each, and 3 tins of fish at K2.25 each cost?
5. I have K20. How much more do I need to buy 10 kg of rice at K14.99 and 3 bottles of cordial at K2.36 each?
6. Which costs more?

   (a) 1 dozen eggs at K3.70, 1 kg onions at K2.99 and 1 L milk at K2.59,

   or

   (b) 1 kg sugar at K2.30, 1 kg potatoes at K2.49 and 1 tin powdered milk at K5.35.
7. How much change will I get from K30 if I buy 3 bottles of tomato sauce at K4.89 each and 3 tins of mixed vegetables at K4.99?
8. I have K50. Do I have enough to buy 2 tins of milk powder at K5.35 each, 10 kg of rice for K15.25, a 6 pack of drink at K3.99, 5 packets of mosquito coils at K1.29 per packet, and 3 kg of beef mince at K7.99 per kilo?
9. I have K10. How much change will I get if I buy a bottle of bleach at K2.47, a bar of soap at K2.98 and a scrubbing brush for K3.21?
10. I want to buy a bottle of sauce at K5.29, a packet of rice at K2.06, a tin of fish for K2.98 and a packet of tea for K2.47. I only have K10. What items can I buy to leave me with the smallest amount of change?